The Mysteries
Of
Spiritual Warfare

Daniel Buraimo

Table of Contents

Foreword

The world's youth have a word to say in these last days and their perception translates to simple attentiveness toward discovering hidden treasures among them. Prophetically, we are in the last days and these are the moments when God needs young people the most. He will use the youth for the glory of His name. All of this, the Prophet Joel has foretold (**Joel 2: 28**)

God needs the intelligence of the youth. He requires their skills, their strength, their vitality, their availability, their courage, their abnegation, their zeal, their endurance, their reflexes, their speed, their insight, and their submission to their predecessors and spiritual authorities to accomplish His plan in this world that is dying immersed in leprosy and the mud of sin.

The essential desire expressed in the pages of this book is that all humanity becomes aware of the existence of the Kingdom of God and Hell and be on God's side to inherit His salvation! But that cannot be done without a real awareness in relation to spiritual warfare and victory that God has given us.

This book speaks of God's plan for man from creation until the end of time, but in reality, it's about spiritual warfare; hence the title, "**THE MYSTERIES OF SPIRITUAL WARFARE**".

People can say without doubt that many authors have already developed this theme, and to this, I will answer, "Repetition is educational." Moreover, a book that talks about Jesus and spiritual warfare should be welcomed.

DANIEL STEEL supports this opinion, "It takes a lot of men to explore a continent; countless people to describe the impenetrable riches of Christ."

Our goal will be achieved if every child of God engages in this warfare as we wait daily for the return of our Master Jesus.

Deacon ANGHUY ADOLPHE-MICHEL

Dedication

I dedicate this book to my twin brother Prophet B. Arnaud Dézoua, my spiritual children who were indulgent when I was writing, and finally, to all readers thirsty for the truth throughout the entire world.

The Mysteries
Of
Spiritual Warfare

Introduction

We believe it is time that every child of God- regardless of where he or she lives- is to become aware of the existence of spiritual warfare and its importance. We have indeed noticed that, in every family, in every house, in every neighborhood, city or village, and even in some countries we have had the grace to visit, there was real warfare, but it is spiritual order. There are spiritual entities (spirits) that control the geographic space and air. They keep families mired in distress and desolation. The atmosphere in these places is so heavy and weird! Spiritual warfare becomes inevitable as one must chase these spirits to bring a true deliverance. They want to keep their subject captive!

It is rightly said by the apostle Paul, "For our struggle is not against flesh and blood, but against the rulers, against the authorities, against the powers of this dark world and against the spiritual forces of evil in the heavenly realms." **(Ephesians 6:12 New International Version)**

Are you aware of existing practices to bewitch, captivate, kill, and render impotent or naive a person without the need of going to their houses or even seeing their face? Do you know there are parents who murder their wives, husbands, children, or relatives to solve their health problems, get out of poverty, or to have some power and authority in their camp? All these things are done in the spirit through certain rites or practices they have mastered! This is approved by their master; the Devil. They can take a statue and invoke the name of the person they want to hurt. If such person is without divine protection, his "soul" will enter the statue. From there, the subject will do what the invoker has set out and programmed them to do. For example, the invoker can kill the person by pressing a needle into the chest/heart of the statue. Once blood flows, it is mission accomplished! Without divine intervention or God's grace, no earthly cardiologist can heal such a trauma. It originates in the spiritual world.

A "hunter" sometimes called "Dozo" (in the language of the Ivory Coast referring to the traditional hunters who have some powers), will shoot in the air shouting the name of a person. If he turns down his gun and blood flows from its end, it is finished—the person whose name was invoked will die because he has been attacked in the spiritual world. Should we seek to remain ignorant as all these atrocities and wicked deeds unfold? No. Awareness vis-à-vis this battle is crucial, the average age is past, and humanity has already experienced the century of enlightenment. Thus, this light must illuminate all aspects of our lives. Ignoring this has serious consequences; refusing information is even worse because it is information that brings transformation and change! Is this not the reason **Hosea 4:6** says, "My people are destroyed for lack of knowledge."? Note it is not God Who refuses to teach us, but rather, we who reject such teachings. "Because you have rejected knowledge, I also reject you as my priests; because you have ignored the law of your God, I also will ignore your children."

However, where did the spiritual warfare begin? What are the weapons that God has placed at our disposal? Furthermore, are we protected against all these enemies? What will be the end of everything, or where is this world heading to? Finally, what is God's plan?

To these questions, we will try to bring elements of responses to inform the children of God.

As you read, strive to reject ignorance for it is too constraining. In the words of philosopher René Descartes, "Only knowledge can make us free." It is liberating knowledge that we will discover through the lines in this work.

Daniel Buraimo

Chapter 1
The Origin of Spiritual Warfare

Spiritual warfare clearly started somewhere. We believe without doubt, through the binding Word of God, that it indeed began in Heaven. Satan (also called Lucifer, the old serpent, or the dragon) was in Heaven with God as a cantor for the glory of God; the Creator, the Almighty, the Absolute, the Lord of the Universe.

But one day, because of his beauty, magnificence, and splendid voice, Satan committed a grievous sin. He attempted to establish his throne above that of God and be like the Most High **(Isaiah 14: 13-14, Ezekiel 28: 13-17)** However, it is important to know that our God does not share His glory, **"I am the Lord; that is my name! I will not yield my glory to another or my praise to idols." (Isaiah 42:8)**

Because the devil was seeking this glory, one understands automatically that a battle was inevitable. This is indeed what the Bible reveals to us, "Then war broke out in heaven. Michael and his angels fought against the dragon, and the dragon and his angels fought back." **(Revelation 12:7)** However, we must recognize that our God could not Himself fight in this battle. He is a God of order! There was an angel established in His army; Michael. It was he who fought against the one who initiated the "coup d'état"—Satan—who was ultimately defeated. Satan was defeated in heaven (where the spiritual battle began) and therefore could stay no longer, "But he was not strong enough, and they lost their place in heaven." **(Revelation 12:8)** It was from there that his downfall started.

The Fall of Satan

As soon as Satan was cast down, he had a dizzying fall. Behold the beginning of the misfortune of the human race because he who was cast down, even at all costs, must land somewhere. This place was Earth, the abode of men, "The great dragon was hurled down—that ancient serpent called the devil, or Satan, who leads the whole world astray. He was hurled to the earth, and his angels with him." **(Revelation 12:9)**

"How you have fallen from heaven, morning star, son of the dawn! You have been cast down to the earth, you who once laid low the nations!!" **(Isaiah 14:12)**

"Your heart became proud on account of your beauty, and you corrupted your wisdom because of your splendor. So I threw you to the earth; I made a spectacle of you before kings." **(Ezekiel 28:17)**

From that moment, heaven and earth had two different pictures! Indeed, while the sky was delighted for the fall of the devil, the world was in tears, "Therefore rejoice, you heavens and you who dwell in them! But woe to the earth and the sea, because the devil has gone down to you! He is filled with fury, because he knows that his time is short." **(Revelation 12:12)**

You know that human behavior is similar to smoke in that, even if hidden or covered by a piece of cloth, it will eventually be revealed. Thus, Satan would set to continue on Earth what he started in Heaven. This world indeed became, "the valley of the shadow of death" **(Psalm 23:4)** The men to whom God has promised longevity ("With long life I will satisfy him and show him my salvation." **(Psalm 91: 16)**) would start dying in the prime of their life. Wars would break out here and there. Brothers and sisters would tear each other apart as they lived in a climate of hatred, mistrust, and intolerance that settled in their hearts. Incurable diseases and epidemics would gain ground. All of this would lead to an unbearable atmosphere, not only for the men themselves, but for God, the Creator! However, He would not remain silent. He would intervene, of course, after making an observation.

The Bitter Observation Made by God And His Intervention

The Bitter Observation Made by God

Man is released to sin by choosing to cooperate with the devil. Indeed, since Satan's fall and his arrival on Earth, he has started working to fill his kingdom. His first victims are undoubtedly our ancestors Adam and Eve; who he led to disobedience by convincing them to eat the fruit of the forbidden tree. This was the original sin! **(Genesis 3)**

It is necessary to draw our attention to a fundamental fact; Satan works extensively with the 'system of doubt' in spiritual warfare. He disguises himself by taking the form of an angel of light, using a soft voice to communicate with our minds. And if we lack vigilance, he will get us! The devil does not come first with horns to scare. He is very subtle and his entire plan is to make men doubt the promises of God. This 'system of doubt' led Adam and Eve out of the plan of the Creator, "Now the serpent was more crafty than any of the wild animals the LORD God had made. He said to the woman, "Did God really say, 'You must not eat from any tree in the garden'?" The woman said to the serpent, "We may eat fruit from the trees in the garden, but God did say, 'You must not eat fruit from the tree that is in the middle of the garden, and you must not touch it, or you will die.'"

"You will not certainly die," the serpent said to the woman. "For God knows that when you eat from it your eyes will be opened, and you will be like God, knowing good and evil." **(Genesis 3:1-5)**

The 'system of doubt' in spiritual warfare lad our ancestors to lose their glory. They listened to the wiles of the devil and they were trapped, "When the woman saw that the fruit of the tree was good for food and pleasing to the eye, and also desirable for gaining wisdom, she took some and ate it. She also gave some to her husband, who was with her, and he ate it." **(Verse 6)** The aim of the devil had been reached; keep the man far from God to make him suffer, "Then the man and his wife heard the sound of the LORD God as he was walking in the garden in the cool of the day, and they hid from the LORD God among the trees of the garden. " **(Verse 8)** But the LORD God called to the man, "Where are you?" **(Verse 9)**

He is asking us the same question today; where are we? With God or the devil? Here, we must respond to God since neutrality has no place in this time. We must have discernment to better locate and cast out the devil but especially receive the power to dwell under the shelter of the Most High. This is what Jesus did when Satan came to Him to tempt Him after forty days and forty nights of fasting. Jesus knew that He was the Son of God, but the tempter approached Him with the same 'system of doubt', **"If you are the Son of God..." (Luke 4:3)** —so that he could defeat Him as he did with Adam and Eve.

But glory be to God because Jesus did not fall for that game. Moreover, by adopting sin, man automatically lost the glory of God, "for all have sinned and fall short of the glory of God," **(Romans 3:23)** The immediate consequence is that he started behaving like his new master. And men, as they multiplied, had nothing of God in them.

The observation made by the Creator is logical, "The LORD saw how great the wickedness of the human race had become on the earth, and that every inclination of the thoughts of the human heart was only evil all the time. The LORD regretted that he had made human beings on the earth, and his heart was deeply troubled." **(Genesis 6:5-6)**

But what will He do?

God's Intervention

In this affliction, God's intervention was rigorous and His decision was firm, "So the LORD said, 'I will wipe from the face of the earth the human race I have created — and with them the animals, the birds and the creatures that move along the ground — for I regret that I have made them.'" **(Genesis 6:7)**

So God sent the flood for forty days **(Genesis 7:17)** and the consequence was disastrous, "Every living thing that moved on land perished — birds, livestock, wild animals, all the creatures that swarm over the earth, and all mankind." **(Genesis 7:21)**

But God had a deep love hidden in His heart for the human race. And He would give His grace to a man named Noah, "But Noah found favor in the eyes of the LORD." **(Genesis 6:8)**

This grace prevented the disappearance of the human race completely from the face of the earth after the flood. Eight people were saved.

God left Noah, the man who made the ark, his wife, their three sons- Shem, Ham and Japheth, - and their wives. God pronounced the same blessing and mandate

He had pronounced on Adam and Eve onto these people, "Then God blessed Noah and his sons, saying to them, "Be fruitful and increase in number and fill the earth." **(Genesis 9:1; 1:28)**

"As for you, be fruitful and increase in number; multiply on the earth and increase upon it." **(Genesis 9:7)**

After this blessing, God would again manifest His love by establishing a covenant with the men that came out of the ark, "God spoke to Noah and his son with him, saying, Behold I establish my covenant with you and with your descendants after you."

What is the substance of this covenant?

"I now establish my covenant with you and with your descendants after you and with every living creature that was with you—the birds, the livestock and all the wild animals, all those that came out of the ark with you— every living creature on earth. I establish my covenant with you: Never again will all life be destroyed by the waters of a flood; never again will there be a flood to destroy the earth." And God said, "This is the sign of the covenant I am making between me and you and every living creature with you, a covenant for all generations to come: I have set my rainbow in the clouds, and it will be the sign of the covenant between me and the earth." **(Genesis 9:9-13)**

After the flood and the coming out of those in the ark, God made another observation. Man has evil thoughts in his heart from his youth, and his heart is deceitful, "Then Noah built an altar to the LORD and, taking some of all the clean animals and clean birds, he sacrificed burnt offerings on it. The LORD smelled the pleasing aroma and said in his heart: 'Never again will I curse the ground because of humans, even though every inclination of the human heart is evil from childhood. And never again will I destroy all living creatures, as I have done.'" **(Genesis 8:20-21)**

"The heart is deceitful above all things and beyond cure. Who can understand it?" **(Jeremiah 17: 9)** Thus, God would opt for a second intervention that was more flexible and required much patience. He would indeed seek to deal with the heart of man by teaching him His Word, "My son, pay attention to what I say; turn your ear to my words. Do not let them out of your sight, keep them within your heart; for they are life to those who find them and health to one's whole body. Above all else, guard your heart, for everything you do flows from it." **(Proverbs 4:20-23)**

"For out of the heart come evil thoughts—murder, adultery, sexual immorality, theft, false testimony, slander." **(Matthew 15:19)**

We may be from the same mother and have different behaviors depending on the state of our heart. We can resemble each other physically and have different spirits like day and night. It is not the outside that makes man—physical beauty is not essential—but rather, the value of the human being is inside. This is what we see a little of in **Luke 6:45,**

"A good man brings good things out of the good stored up in his heart, and an evil man brings evil things out of the evil stored up in his heart. **For the mouth speaks what the heart is full of."**

Daniel Buraimo

Chapter 2
The Deliverance In Spiritual Warfare

To cure a disease, it is important to go to the root. If we go to the root of the problem; we will be able to apply the proper solution without being misled. If we put the cart before the horse, the work will not progress, and we will only be going backwards. We must first diagnose the case in front of us, like the doctor, and then we can prescribe the correct medications. We do not plant on a space without first preparing the soil.

Listen to the prophet **Jeremiah** to whom the Lord gave instructions, "See, today I appoint you over nations and kingdoms to uproot and tear down, to destroy and overthrow, to build and to plant." **(Jeremiah 1:10)**

Before the verbs **'build'** and **'plant'** God speaks **to pull down, kill, destroy, and throw down**! This is deliverance!

It is necessary that the person who appears before us be stripped of what has caused the problem then, once released, they can continually enjoy their life. It is for this reason that the Bible says in **Revelation 2:5,** "Consider how far you have fallen! Repent and do the things you did at first. If you do not repent, I will come to you and remove your lampstand from its place." 'Where you art fallen' is synonymous with the origin, the beginning, or the place where it all began. Once we recognize this, we apply the necessary solution needed and so Satan will no longer have access to our lives.

There is therefore what we call altars that were built in the lives of some people. And on these altars, there are demons that are established and control the lives of these people. We must cast them out- that is to say dethrone them- and then destroy the altars otherwise they will come back; especially if the work of destruction was not done. And after destroying everything, we must build another altar to the Lord our God.

This is what God told Gideon, "That same night the LORD said to him, 'Take the second bull from your father's herd, the one seven years old. Tear down your father's altar to Baal and cut down the Asherah pole beside it. Then build a proper kind of altar to the LORD your God on the top of this height. Using the wood of the Asherah pole that you cut down, offer the second bull as a burnt offering.'" **(Judges 6:25-26)**

If you start this way following the order given by God Himself, I think that the demons cast out will not return nor dare to sit on the altar of praise, worship, prayer, meditation on the Word of God, and dedication that you have built for God. What we often forget is that when cast out, an evil spirit goes, but he comes back later to see if his altar is still there, intact. If this is the case, then he will seek reinforcements, seven other spirits more wicked than himself, to come and settle on the throne where he was dislodged. It is therefore important to destroy the base, the house, the altar, and the dwelling of evil spirits by the name of JESUS and remain in the Lord by building another glorious altar.

What did Jesus tell us in the Gospel of Matthew?

"When an impure spirit comes out of a person, it goes through arid places seeking rest and does not find it. Then it says, 'I will return to the house I left.' When it arrives, it finds the house unoccupied, swept clean and put in order. Then it goes and takes with it seven other spirits more wicked than itself, and they go in and live there. And the final condition of that person is worse than the first. That is how it will be with this wicked generation." **(Chapter 12:43-45)**

May God help us to understand the Holy Scriptures for glory of His name, Amen!

Reveal some altars and destroy them by the power of the Holy Spirit in Jesus' Name!

The Names From Altars

Brothers and sisters, do you know the name you bear may be the source of your problem? Do you know that there are names which automatically call unclean spirits?

And when you bear them, a demon is sent that comes to establish itself on the throne of your life through the altar that was built from this name! This is the great lesson that David received from Abigail when he wanted to lay his hands on Nabal for his wickedness and his ingratitude. She succeeded to convince this man of war by explaining that the origin of the problem of her husband 'NABAL' was his name,

"Please pay no attention, my lord, to that wicked man Nabal. He is just like his name—his name means Fool, and folly goes with him. And as for me, your servant, I did not see the men my lord sent." **(1 Samuel 25:25)**

In the spiritual realm, you need to destroy every altar and dethrone any demon who works through your name. If you want to keep your name on your administrative document, you can. Through praying, you still need to change your name! The idea is to change the name totally.

Jabez had this problem. He resorted to prayer and God changed his destiny for good.

"...his mother called his name Jabez, saying, 'Because I bare him with sorrow.' And Jabez called on the God of Israel, saying, 'Oh that you would bless me indeed, and enlarge my territory, and that your hand might be with me, and that you would keep me from evil, that it may not grieve me!' God granted him that which he requested." **(1 Chronicles 4:9)**

Jabez prayed to God to destroy the throne (or the altar) that his mother erected from the name she gave him. It is appropriate for parents to remember that they should not give any name to their children. Instead, they must choose names that have good meanings; names that have common sense.

From a single name, the life of a person could be destroyed. Naming a person with a word holding negative meaning produces a constant restatement of the negative impact in their life. Now life and death are in our tongue, moreover faith comes from what is heard. Therefore when hearing that name, the demon attacks and destroys the life of the person.

The Yoruba- a people of West Africa living in Nigeria (the country I came from)- give the name 'BABATUNDE' to children born shortly after the death of a father or grandfather. And this name means, "The father returned." This is dangerous, it is an altar. The Bible says, "As a cloud vanishes and is gone, so one who goes down to the grave does not return. He will never come to his house again; his place will know him no more." **(Job 7:9-10)**

Such a child is inhabited by a spirit of death which may occur at any time to shorten his life.

I suggest that if there is possibility to change the name, do it! Those who bear the name of mountains, waters, rivers, stones, or dead relatives must pray a lot for their deliverance and be called by another name. Even if their new name is not on their birth certificate, let them be identified by this new name; this is already good. People call me Daniel although my name, BURAIMO SIMIU, does not cause any problem. Everyone calls me Pastor Daniel.

It is a name I received in a dream after leaving my Muslim parents. I was sleeping when God opened my eyes in the spirit. I was in a large room where someone was preaching. He pointed his finger to me and told me, "You henceforth, you will be called Daniel!"

This is how that name was given to me. God can also give you a name by revelation or by inspiration! Our heavenly Father saw the importance of changing the names of certain people before they entered into their prophetic destiny.

ABRAM saw God change his name, "Neither shall your name any more be called Abram, but your name shall be **ABRAHAM**; for a father of many nations have I made you." **(Genesis 17:5)** It was after deliverance and a change of name that Abraham was able to give birth to the promised son **ISAAC** with his lawful wife **SARAH**.

Do not forget that the name of **SARAH** was also changed by God, "God also said to Abraham, 'As for Sarai your wife, you are no longer to call her Sarai; her name will be Sarah.'" **(Genesis 17:15)** God is declaring that the deliverance has taken place in the life of the man and the woman. We note that it is demonstrated in the lives Abraham and Sarah. If Abraham is the father of nations and required a changing of his name, it could not have been otherwise for Sarah as she is the mother of nations!

JACOB was to be called **ISRAEL**, "Then the man said, 'Your name will no longer be Jacob, but Israel,'" **(Genesis 32:28)** Jacob means deceiver and thief, while Israel means 'people blessed of God.'

SAUL became **PAUL**, the great Apostle. In Acts 9:1-2, Saul breathes hatred and anger against the followers of the doctrine of Christ.

In **Acts 9:17-18**, God visits Saul and his eyes were opened to the truth of the Gospel. Now Paul who was known as Saul, will do exploits unto God in the name of Jesus **(Acts 13: 9)**

SIMON was like a reed shaken by the wind, but Jesus baptized him as Cephas, "And he brought him to Jesus. Jesus looked at him and said, 'You are Simon son of John. You will be called Cephas' (which, when translated, is Peter.)" **(John 1:42)**

He additionally states in **Matthew 16:18,** "And I tell you that you are Peter, and on this rock I will build my church, and the gates of Hades will not overcome it."

Jesus Christ built a glorious altar in Peter's life by changing his name.

Natural fathers or spiritual are tasked with prophesying words on your children from the names you give to them just as God and Jesus did.

Here is a quick reference of Biblical names:

HANNAH: "Grace or Prayer" She had her son Samuel by the grace of God in prayer.

BATHSHEBA: "Daughter of an oath, a covenant." We do not know what oath her parents made but immediately after King David saw her, he desired to go after her. It was she who was later the mother of the great King Solomon. **(2 Samuel 11)**

RUTH: "Friend" She was attached to her mother-in-law Naomi. They were friendly and nothing could separate them, not even the death of their husbands.

NAOMI: "Nice" She advised Ruth until she married Boaz.

SARAH: "Princesses, the mother of nations."

ELISABETH: "Oath of God" The mother of John the Baptist; forerunner of Jesus. He was a great servant of God even until his death.

MARY: "Bitterness" Mary, the mother of Jesus, had to suffer bitterly for her crucified son. Mary, the mother of JAMES, experienced the bitterness when her son was also killed.

ADAM: "Red man" He came out of the earth. His name influenced him. He sinned against God and God told him, "…for dust you are and to dust you will return." **(Genesis 3:19)**

ABEL & CAIN: "Vanity" and CAIN means "Possession." We know the story of two brothers. Cain was no more the master of himself and possessed of a spirit of murder, jealousy, and hatred, killed his brother Abel on the same day **(Genesis 4: 1-8)** Adam and Eve lost their two children "Vanity" and "Possession" as Abel was killed and Cain, was driven away by God.

SAMSON: "Little sun" He shone a little and then later disappeared with the Philistines in the rubble of the wall that he made to fall.

SAMUEL: "Heard of God" He was a powerful prophet in his time and what he said never failed to come to pass.

SAUL: "Asked" the people wanted a king and asked whereas

DAVID: "Loved" Chosen by God. Hence the expression, "The man after God's own heart." Saul, the 'asked' was jealous of David, the 'loved' of God!

NEHEMIAH: "Jehovah console" It was he who built the walls of Jerusalem and it comforted not only the Jews who had returned from exile, but Nehemiah who was grieved by the condition of the walls before reconstruction. (Extracted from Thompson Bible, Pages 1706-1708)

In short, understand that name influences the person who bears it in one way or the other. These few names are meant to edify and demonstrate the importance of naming with purpose.

Altars From the Blood Bond

What of blood ties?

When we talk about blood ties, one must understand that it is the past actions of parents that have influence on the lives of their children. A child may be a victim of something he did not do, he is ignorant! A man who lives in homosexuality, for instance, and eventually marries as well as fathering children should not be surprised to see his children develop an attraction to same-sex peers! Why? Because their genes predisposed them to it. More specifically, their father built an altar that they have simply inherited.

This is what God's Word says,

"And he passed in front of Moses, proclaiming, 'The LORD, the LORD, the compassionate and gracious God, slow to anger, abounding in love and faithfulness, maintaining love to thousands, and forgiving wickedness, rebellion and sin. Yet he does not leave the guilty unpunished; he punishes the children and their children for the sin of the parents to the third and fourth generation.'" **(Exodus 34:6-7)**

The number of years has no influence on blood ties or a curse. It is imperative to break and destroy it in the name of Jesus. Otherwise children will suffer from this, as well as grandchildren and so on.

If you know the story about your family that began a blood tie, go and confess it to an anointed person of God and through prayer, they will break this bondage and the coming generation will be liberated through you. We do not allow a snake to roam in the house where we plan to sleep. We must dislodge it compulsorily.

The curse in your family must stop at your level. Become the terminus of the curse of your family and the beginning of a new, glorious, radiant, and beautiful life.

In villages throughout Africa, there are families that are bonded since colonization, because their ancestors released curses saying that none of their children would succeed in the school of the white in hopes that they would all go back to the village. This is bondage and, at the same time, a curse.

Today, all parents at the edge of 21st century know the importance of education to catapult people out of poverty and expand their ability to improve communities and families. If this bond is not broken and if this curse is not destroyed in the name of Jesus, suffering and failure passed though the children, will always end up returning without completing their studies because of what their parents have said and done.

Remember, in doing so, the original intention of the ancestors was to protect their offspring from, 'the evil settlers' and the ways they treated the blacks! And Yet, the bond is sealed; you should break it now that we are aware of spiritual truths and modern needs.

In addition, there are families where girls do not marry. Whatever the number of women, you will find that they are all single or those who have married, divorced or lost their husbands. You should know that this can be bondage from a disappointment endured by a great mother or an ancestor. Being disappointed by men in all her relationships, she declared that no drop of blood will suffer what she has suffered. They may have friends, and lovers, but no marriage lest they suffer. The words act as an altar, and it's a link to be broken.

Blood ties are the emanation of our acts. An act today can become a blood link tomorrow. There is a family that suffers today because every child born outside of the village dies while those born in the village specifically on a large shed, stay alive. Indeed, it was at the time of slavery and a slave became pregnant. While she was laboring, they put her on the shed but thank God, the shed was very solid. And there on the branches of trees covered with straw, she gave birth to her child. She asked her mistress why she was made to suffer such atrocities?

"It is to avoid you absconding after giving birth."

The slave began to weep and said, "Every woman in this family or married to a man of this family will not embrace her child except if she comes to give birth where I have given birth."

They thought it was a joke.

It wasn't until after they observed that all the women lost their children after giving birth that they realized the curse pronounced by the slave became a bond within the family. And indeed, all that gave birth on the shed as a slave kept their child.

Do not play with bonds; they must be broken in the name of Jesus and after a good repentance. See a biblical event with our father in faith, Abraham. He is the friend of God and father of faith, but be careful, there was a bond in his life and in the lives of his children after him. It was Abraham who committed the act which led to this bond. In **Genesis 20:1-5**, we read how Abraham had "lied" to Abimelec, king of Gerar, telling him that his wife Sarah was his sister to preserve his life because his wife was very beautiful!

And in Genesis 26:6-10, Isaac, the son of Abraham, would say the same sentence over his wife Rebecca, "She is my sister." The reasons were the same; she was beautiful as well, so he said it to preserve his life. The altar was built, the bond had been sealed, it must be broken and destroyed.

Isaac, the father of Jacob **(Genesis 25:21-34)** saw his son not only deceive him but also steal the birthright owed to his elder brother Esau, **(verses 31-33)** so he could snatch the blessing he was to deliver to the elder. **(Genesis 27:22-23)** The bond of blood takes effect. Jacob could not stay with his family; he had to save his life by fleeing under the threat of a brother who he had supplanted twice, "And he said, is not he rightly named Jacob? for he hath supplanted me these two times: he took away my birthright; and, behold, now he hath taken away my blessing… and Esau said in his heart, The days of mourning for my father are at hand; then will I slay my brother Jacob." (Verses 36-41) Having heard the news through his mother, Jacob found himself in the house of his maternal uncle Laban, the brother of his mother, Rebecca. Thus, he was conscious of the spiritual journey! A journey that does not begin when everything goes well but when death approaches; when danger is in the horizon!

The distance does not affect the blood bond; there must be deliverance in the Name of Jesus and by the Word of God. At Laban's, Jacob, by deceit, becomes the owner of strong sheep leaving only the feeble to his uncle who later became his father-in-law. **(Genesis 30:37-43)** And even on his departure, he did not inform his stepfather, "Moreover, Jacob deceived Laban the Aramean by not telling him he was running away. So he fled with all he had, crossed the Euphrates River, and headed for the hill country of Gilead." **(Genesis 31:20-21)**

It is in this fight that God, in His sovereignty, decides to change the prophetic destiny of Jacob. In chapter 32 of Genesis, Moses makes us understand that Jacob wrestled with a man until daybreak. This bout was worth the effort, because the links had to be broken so that Jacob could assert himself. You cannot escape this fight as long as there is a family bond, parental bond, or a blood bond.

Jacob took advantage of the fight to ask for his total deliverance and he got it, "And Jacob said, 'I will not let you go, except you bless me.' The man discerned that this descendant of Abraham was a carrier of a great future but threatened by the blood bond that was attached to his name. So he said to him, 'What is your name?'

'Jacob.'"

This is where his story would know a change. "Thy name shall be called no more Jacob, but Israel: for as a prince, you have power with God and with men, and has prevailed."

It is after the deliverance that Jacob will receive the blessing.

"And Jacob asked him, and said, 'Tell me, I pray you, your name.' And he said, 'Wherefore is it that you ask after my name?' And he blessed him there."

God confirms this blessing in **Genesis 35:10-12**, "God said to him, 'Your name is Jacob, but you will no longer be called Jacob; your name will be Israel.' So he named him Israel. And God said to him, 'I am God Almighty; be fruitful and increase in number. A nation and a community of nations will come from you, and kings will be among your descendants. The land I gave to Abraham and Isaac I also give to you, and I will give this land to your descendants after you.'"

I prophesy that any bond that follows you and all blood ties be broken in the Name of Jesus. You shall enter as Jacob into your blessing.

Amen!

Altars From Worship

When we speak of worship, it's all worship given to creations at the expense of the Creator. God does not need us to call upon him from His creation; He wants us to pray to Him directly. The worship therefore made to gods like water, mountains, stones, trees, or cults to idols, are an abomination before God.

"They exchanged the truth about God for a lie, and worshiped and served created things rather than the Creator—who is forever praised. Amen." **(Romans 1:25)**

It is painful to see the children of God deliver their souls to the devil via horrible practices. There are even intellectuals who get naked in the forest or in the water, repeating phrases that they don't understand. And all this to glorify Satan, the father of lies. By doing this, they're attracting the wrath of God upon themselves and on their children that they are quoting before their new master; the devil! They will enter into termite mounds to force the door of elevation. This is spiritual prostitution and it is adultery. I do not think your god whom you worship can save you before the anger and jealousy of our Father Creator, **"Do not worship any other god, for the LORD, whose name is Jealous, is a jealous God."** (Exodus 34:14)

"You shall not make for yourself an image in the form of anything in heaven above or on the earth beneath or in the waters below. You shall not bow down to them or worship them; for I, the LORD your God, am a jealous God, punishing the children for the sin of the parents to

the third and fourth generation of those who hate me,"
(Exodus 20:4-5)

God says categorically in verse 3, "**You shall have no other gods before me**." By disobeying this word through the worship of other gods, you are trying to build altars to demons not only for you but also for your children and your grandchildren. The demons you invoke in your worship will begin to control your life and that of your descendants, and in the end, your life will be as dark as a starless night.

Remember this lesson: The devil gives with the right hand and snatches with the left hand. However, you can always get rid of these spirits by giving your life to Jesus. You know these demons follow the worshiper, following the things that are have devoted to the user. Only the name of Jesus can really deliver you from all this suffering and spiritual bondage!

Leave the modern idolatry which replaced the traditional, they are all the same. In short, cut off with all these things, and give glory and honor to the ONLY AND TRUE GOD.

The Transfer of Spirits

The transfer of spirits is done in many ways, and man can easily contact demons if he is not careful. Every day in society, terrible things happen. People ignorantly receive a lot of evil spirits in their lives through their behaviors, practices, and actions. Transfer of spirits occurs when spirits leave the body of a living being to seek refuge in another body. We are told this reality by Evangelist Mark,

"They went across the lake to the region of the Gerasenes. When Jesus got out of the boat, a man with an impure spirit came from the tombs to meet him. This man lived in the tombs, and no one could bind him anymore, not even with a chain. For he had often been chained hand and foot, but he tore the chains apart and broke the irons on his feet. No one was strong enough to subdue him. Night and day among the tombs and in the hills he would cry out and cut himself with stones. When he saw Jesus from a distance, he ran and fell on his knees in front of him. He shouted at the top of his voice, "What do you want with me, Jesus, Son of the Most High God? In God's name don't torture me!" For Jesus had said to him, "Come out of this man, you impure spirit!" Then Jesus asked him, "What is your name?" "My name is Legion," he replied, "for we are many." And he begged Jesus again and again not to send them out of the area. A large herd of pigs was feeding on the nearby hillside. The demons begged Jesus, "Send us among the pigs; allow us to go into them." He gave them permission, and the impure spirits came out and went into the pigs. The herd, about two thousand in number, rushed down the steep bank into the lake and were drowned." **(Mark 5:1-13)**

What we call the transfer of spirits is what you just read, "And the unclean spirits **went out** and **entered** the swine." This scenario is seen every day in our society. These words you read or that you hear deliver you in the name of Jesus!

A child of God does not eat from anywhere, nor from just any people because through food, drink, or whatever may enter into your mouth, many people have contracted spirits that eventually destroy their lives. Always sanctify your meal with the blood of Jesus before eating, even if it is prepared by someone you have absolute confidence in. Never put anything in your mouth without sanctifying it.

The devil rode, he does not play, he seeks to devour. There is a brother whom I prayed for because he was having a cough that stressed him a lot. And the brother had a gift of deliverance for God anointed him in this area. And during the prayer, the Lord opened my eyes on the origin of this disease: He took a biscuit from a sister in faith after service. The spirit took the opportunity to install the cough in his throat.

Admittedly, one can fall sick without spiritual influence, but I tell you that the brother dragged it for a long time despite all care. The unclean spirits did not want him to continue to pray as his prayer was fatal to them, so they had to stop him. Brothers and sisters, let us be simple as a dove, but wise as serpents. (**Matthew 10:16**)

There are restaurants or places where you do not feel at ease and your soul refuses to eat. Do not insist and do not eat to please anyone. The food goes into your blood, so be careful!

One day, while I was still a student, a woman that I knew very well invoked the spirits of the dead on the food she brought for me. The Spirit told me that day not to break my fast but to continue fasting until the following day. Disobedience deserves punishment and this is what happened to me. I ate this bad food, which tasted quite pleasant in the natural world.

I quickly felt very bad, lost consciousness and was powerless, confused, looking distant. I prayed my various warfare and restoration prayers before and I fell asleep. In the night, I had a dream and was told, "You ate death whereas we need you for a great ministry. You must therefore fast for eighteen days consecutively to destroy all the seeds of premature death you have eaten."

I fasted and on the eighteenth day, I dreamed of vomiting throughout the night. This vomit was dark; it had nothing to do with what I ate in the visible world.

When I woke up, I realized many things because I was wet as if I was dipped in water. It was transfer of spirits through food. May God deliver us from the hand of the wicked, and free us from any natural or spiritual food prepared to do us evil.

Through the 'touch' one can contract or exchange demons. A man possessed by evil spirits can pass it by simple greetings; either by the fact of shaking of hands, or by kisses.

How many women have found themselves in the arms of men they never loved because they simply shook their hand and vice-versa?

Understand the importance of always praying for protection. There are people who come to congratulate relatives or friends who just had a child, by taking the child or touching his head or cheek or any part of the body. Such people communicate a spirit to children to destroy their future. You know that every child born comes with a star, and there are people who see and plan to fight against these stars.

They cannot kill the child physically, the society is guaranteed by laws, so they do it spiritually.

Parents, open your eyes and be vigilant coverers of your child. Cover them with the blood of Jesus. With this knowledge, do not allow just anyone to shave the hair of your newly born, to bathe him, or to give him drink. And you must take care of the umbilical cord. Take it yourself on the day it will fall. And moreover, it has to be people you are sure of to take the placenta as soon as the child is born into the world. All these things are important because outside of prayer, we must be watchful, says the Word of God. It is the future of your children and yourself.

When we speak of transfer of spirits by 'touch', it covers several areas. It is about everything we give or receive as well as everything that touches our hands or our body. It can be clothes, shoes, a well-packaged gift, or even a car. Whether you give it or receive it, always dip these things in the Blood of Jesus. If there is a spirit behind it, it can never stand the Blood of Jesus. Even if spirits do not die, they will be suffocated by the blood of the Lamb. This is to remind you that if you lose something that is as close as your toothbrush, your underwear, your singlet, towel or even your ointment and after the disappearance, these things come back as if by magic, do not use them anymore! There may be danger because spirits may have been invoked to accomplish evil things in your life. As long as you are distracted, it is finished!

Caution is biblical, do not tempt God. **(Matthew 10:16)**

An unconverted relative lost his sandals and three days later, found them at the entrance to his room. Without asking questions, he put them on his feet. It was as good farewell to the world! He died with swollen feet screaming horribly in pain! May God save us from such things in the name of Jesus!

Also, when there are accidents and people die, the spirit of death is already present; he prepares the next victims. Being in the place and seeing a relative or friend, do not throw yourself on the corpse in any way. By touching it, there can be a transfer of spirits and you risk carrying a spirit of death while alive. If nothing is done for you to be delivered, the day when the spirit wakes up as a Leviathan will mark your last day as he will take you! Always ask for the protection of God before handling an accident-involved corpse. May the Lord preserve us from premature death in the Name of Jesus!

There are too many demons that we receive through ignorance, even in the house of God. I mean the *laying of hands* specifically. In **Mark 16:17-18** the Bible says, "And these signs will accompany those who believe: In my name they will drive out demons; they will speak in new tongues; they will pick up snakes with their hands; and when they drink deadly poison, it will not hurt them at all; they will place their hands on sick people, and they will get well."

This suggests that he who is laying his hand, believes in God, and is filled with the Holy Spirit who enables him to transmit healing by the laying of hands. But if it is not the case, he can contract a demon or transmit one. There are times when the Lord will ask us not to lay hands on people, until we have had a real conversation with them.

There are several categories of demons that the devil sends with the intent to make people sick, weaken them, or make the servants of God that disturb them fall.

Those who perform deliverance for the Lord must ask God to grant them discernment and open their spiritual eyes! A brother in Christ fell into a coma while he was doing deliverance. At the Health center, doctors after diagnosis found a deep infection in his head; internal hemorrhaging as if he had an accident! Never had this brother had accident in the natural world. The transfer of spirits is a reality. The day you are not prepared, do not lay hands. Hear the voice of the Spirit before acting.

The Apostle Paul understood these things when he said to his spiritual son Timothy, "Do not be hasty in the laying on of hands, and do not share in the sins of others. Keep yourself pure." **(1 Timothy 5:22)**

The laying of hands has become a fashion and if it is not done, the people think they are not blessed! What do we do with the power of the Word? May God help us!

The transfer of spirits is also done through *sex*. It is here that Satan strikes many people who do not know the realities of spiritual warfare. Do not have sex in just any way or with just anybody. We do not know who is who and who does what. There are moments when the demons need your blood to reach you in some aspect of your life. And they possess a girl or a man, who embodies your preferred style and taste, that they place along your way. Once sexual intercourse takes place, the spirits take hold of your blood and enter your body to quietly do their work according to the order they received from their master, the devil. Either they make you sick, weaken you, destroy your finances, or they kill you outright.

Do you know that the devil has a lot of girls he has possessed on earth? They are secured for a special mission!

There is a spirit called the 'queen of heaven' who is a very powerful spirit that traffics in seduction. Few people are able to resist her charm. Be careful, she is the poison on the diamond, she is a snake with deadly poison and a monster in sheep's clothing. Whoever drinks the wine of her fornication gets drunk and cannot be detached from her except God intervenes by his servants in the Name of Jesus.

This is how she destroyed many homes, where a man no longer sees his wife as a woman, he no longer feels any pleasure with his wife as all his thoughts are outside his home. It is reciprocal for the women.

Brothers and sisters be careful, the devil roams about. His only intention is to devour. When the demon came down to the earth, he devastated everything because man loved what is sweet to his palate, and did not think about the consequences. People in authority or men and women in business are the target of these evil spirits. Their goal is to lead the leaders into immorality.

What does the Word of God say? "Babylon the great is fallen, is fallen, and is become the habitation of devils, and the hold of every foul spirit, and a cage of every unclean and hateful bird. For all nations have drunk of the wine of the wrath of her fornication, and the kings of the earth have committed fornication with her, and the merchants of the earth are waxed rich through the abundance of her delicacies."

The word of God is clear and precise. It gives you advice people of God, "Then I heard another voice from heaven say: 'Come out of her, my people,' so that you will not share in her sins, so that you will not receive any of her plagues" **(Revelation 18:4)** There is no alternative! Get out of this sin if you want to come out. Invoke the fire of God to burn her; this queen who sits in your life or control your home. Pray aggressive prayers and save your home, save your husband, save your wife or your children from her clutches. She is not a spirit that romances with dead prayers, "Give her as much torment and grief as the glory and luxury she gave herself. In her heart she boasts, 'I sit enthroned as queen. I am not a widow; I will never mourn.'" **(Revelation 18:7)**

Such is her determination. But you will also decree a thing, and it shall be established unto you to dislodge her. **(Job 22:28)** For the Word is precise, "She will be consumed by fire, for mighty is the Lord God who judges her." **(Revelation 18:8)**

I pray that the Lord God release you from this spirit, by the fire of the Holy Spirit in the Name of Jesus! Amen!

However, it is important to destroy all the altars we built into our lives by intercourse we have had before marriage. We must do it one after the other. The Holy Spirit will remind you so that you have a good deliverance. You can do it with God's anointed or have a self-deliverance. Do not play with it. They must do it because our lives often revolve around the first person with whom we had intercourse. From there, our lives may be affected forever. Satan uses sex in spiritual warfare to foundationally affect the lives and destroy the futures of many people. This is the case for HIV & AIDS, which we know the damage and devastation across the world.

Pray this prayer with me:

"Lord, forgive all sins that I have committed through sex in the name of Jesus. Wash me with Your Precious Blood and sanctify me. Lord God, I destroy and I consume with Your fire every altar built in my life through intimate relationships that I had with X (the name of the person or the names of the different people) in the name of Jesus.

All traces and spiritual consequences that are left in my life, and are acting negatively be erased completely by the Blood of Jesus Christ,

Amen! "

Moreover, when we reference the transfer of spirits, there are several cases. We cannot list them all for the sake of comprehensive coverage, but it is up to everyone to ensure they watch over their lives and practices to avoid falling to a demonic yoke.

By television and by some movies, you can contact a spirit that will lead to acting according to what has been seen. A child may want to imitate what he saw on television or in a movie and in doing so, there is often damage.

How many children have committed incest, injured a brother or sister, or stole from their parents simply because there was a transfer of spirits through the television?

At one point, a spirit of violence possessed the children and many have fractured bodies because they wanted to resemble 'Tarzan' by jumping from one tree to another!

There are also those who defile their spirit by reading and meditating with occult books. They buy expensive books to connect to Satan. This is serious!

I advise you to burn them as it was done with the first Christians in **Acts 19:19**. This is the same thing for certain decorations, frames, or certain objects considered artwork that are controlled by spirits. They are likely to create lot of problems in the family or in the home. Behind the beauty, decoration, and utility, the spirits are there. They see everything, hear everything, and take control to destroy all good projects.

Be very careful with paintings of the Egyptian as well as some Japanese art works; some African masks are not to be trifled with either. I recommend that we burn them rather than give them as gifts or sell them, regardless of the amount, "**Many of them also used curious arts brought their books together, and burned them before all men: and they counted the price of them, and found it fifty thousand pieces of silver.**" It was expensive, but they agreed to burn them.

Why should we burn them? Because we must not in a spirit of love, create problems of spiritual order for people to whom they are given or to whom they are sold, but also because the Word of God gives us this example to follow.

May the Lord bless us, make us understand these mysteries, and make us spiritual women and men. Amen!

Chapter 3
The Weapons
of Spiritual Warfare

When we talk about spiritual warfare, it is not a child's play, a fable, or chimeras but a fight, a battle, a confrontation between us and the evil forces. This is to say no to the devil, refusing that darkness should govern our lives, and to take back properties that we have lost. We sit on our seat, dress well, eat well, sleep, and prosper through our work. Brief success as God wants on earth before even going to heaven.

We are not the result of a chance! Our life on earth identifies and concerns God and He has prepared everything for our success, **"For I know the plans I have for you," declares the LORD, "plans to prosper you and not to harm you, plans to give you hope and a future." (Jeremiah 29:11)**

We were spirit before living in a physical body. This is what God was trying to explain to Jeremiah who refused His prophetic call, "Before I formed you in the womb I knew you, before you were born I set you apart; I appointed you as a prophet to the nations." **(Jeremiah 1:5)** This implies that each of us has a specific mission to accomplish on Earth. It is the mission God the Almighty, the Creator of all things had engraved on the table of our mind.

An example much more revealing can be seen in the book of **Judges 13:1-5**, "Again the Israelites did evil in the eyes of the LORD, so the LORD delivered them into the hands of the Philistines for forty years. 2 A certain man of Zorah, named Manoah, from the clan of the Danites, had a wife who was childless, unable to give birth. 3 The angel of the LORD appeared to her and said, "You are barren and childless, but you are going to become pregnant and give birth to a son. 4 Now see to it that you drink no wine or other fermented drink and that you do not eat anything unclean. 5 You will become pregnant and have a son whose head is never to be touched by a razor **because the boy is to be a Nazirite, dedicated to God from the womb. He will take the lead in delivering Israel from the hands of the Philistines."**

Here is a man to whom God wanted to give a specific mission that is the beginning of the deliverance of Israel from the Philistines. But what is wonderful is that before the child is conceived in the womb of his mother, God through the mouth of the angel, had given the prophecy about his life on earth. In the same way, there is a prophecy concerning you from God. You are a star shining somewhere and God's desire is that His wonderful plan is fulfilled in your life and you are happy, "A man may have a hundred children and live many years; yet no matter how long he lives, if he cannot enjoy his prosperity and does not receive proper burial, I say that a stillborn child is better off than he." **(Ecclesiastes 6:3)**

Therefore, anything that can prevent your evolution- anyone working in the invisible world against what will bring you joy and happiness- is your opponent. They are agents of the devil and you have to fight them so that you can enter into your prophetic destiny and serve your God; otherwise a miscarriage would be happier than you. We must recognize to face invisible enemies, our weapons must also be invisible. In spiritual warfare, spiritual weapons are indispensable, "Finally, be strong in the Lord and in his mighty power. Put on the full armor of God, so that you can take your stand against the devil's schemes." **(Ephesians 6:10-11)**

We need to be armed with the weapons of God; weapons given by God! Why? To stand firm against the wiles of the devil. For the natural man loves what strikes the eye,

"Finally, be strong in the Lord and in his mighty power. 11 Put on the full armor of God, so that you can take your stand against the devil's schemes." **(1 Samuel 16:7)**

Do not look at the charms, amulets, rings, magic powder, or the cowries that strike the eyes; the devil is ingenious in evil. Rather fix your eyes on God and use the weapons that He has given for spiritual warfare. Then you will have victory over the devil.

What are these weapons? Let us study some of them together.

The Name of Jesus

The name of Jesus is a powerful weapon in spiritual warfare. This is the name that God gave us to destroy demonic forces and powers of darkness, "For God so loved the world that he gave his one and only Son, that whoever believes in him shall not perish but have eternal life." **(John 3:16)**

The birth of Jesus, and His coming into the world had a specific purpose; He came to the earth to finish the battle He started in heaven. If Satan came down to earth after being cast down and the earth is under his dominion then a day must come for the deliverance!

"The devil led him up to a high place and showed him in an instant all the kingdoms of the world. And he said to him, "I will give you all their authority and splendor; it has been given to me, and I can give it to anyone I want to.'" **(Luke 4:5-6)** "The thief comes only to steal and kill and destroy; I have come that they may have life, and have it to the full." **(John 10:10)**

Jesus Gives Life

To understand better the salvation mission of Jesus, it is important to start with Genesis, the book of origins,

"This is the account of the heavens and the earth when they were created, when the LORD God made the earth and the heavens."

"Then the LORD God formed a man from the dust of the ground and **breathed into his nostrils the breath of life, and the man became a living being." (Genesis 2:4,7)** Without going into certain considerations, accept here man is bipartisan, meaning man is made of body (the dust earth) and spirit (breath of life) It is this spirit that makes us worshipers of God for, "God is spirit, and his worshipers must worship in the Spirit and in truth." **(John 4:24)** We can understand then while Satan is unleashed, he always seeks to destroy the spirit; the most important part of the human being, "But it is the spirit in a person, the breath of the Almighty, that gives them understanding." **(Job 32:8)**

The tragedy is that Satan could imprison our minds and his plan was to lead us in a starless night that would not follow any day, where there is no glimmer of hope! This is what happened in the Garden of Eden when Adam and Eve ate the forbidden fruit. They did not die physically, but spiritually they were separated from communion with God.

The Almighty God and Omnipresent did not see Adam spiritually speaking, he was 'forced' to ask him, "Adam, where are you?" **(Genesis 3:1-9)** This is how far the devil leads us all without exception, "For all have sinned and come short of the glory of God." **(Romans 3:23)**

In this confusion, and to cover his nakedness, the man will make belts with fig leaves having discovered that he was naked after eaten the forbidden fruit. **(Genesis 3:7)**

This is what we see today.

Men made all kinds of religious garments, and they think they are right! But how long will fig leaves protect us? Then God will grant man another solid suit so that he can be protected against the elements of nature,

"The LORD God made garments of skin for Adam and his wife and clothed them." **(Genesis 3:21)** To save Adam and his wife, the animal that was sacrificed symbolizes for us Jesus who stands as the Lamb of God, "Look, Lamb of God…" **(John 1:29)** It was sent from heaven to put an end to the works of the devil and to stop us from the path of eternal perdition where Satan led us with all these religions without salvation! **Jesus Christ came to give us salvation, eternal life**! This is what is most important to God!

The devil can present to us the glory of the world and its beauty, all the wealth that we desire, but these things cannot guarantee our salvation, "What good will it be for someone to gain the whole world, yet forfeit their soul? Or what can anyone give in exchange for their soul?" **(Matthew 16:26)**

Our soul has value before God that is to be saved first and other things will follow, "**But seek first his kingdom and his righteousness, and all these things will be given to you as well.**" **(Matthew 6:33)** Do not let the devil deceive us, everything is ours! But accept this fatal weapon that is the name of Jesus first. The name of Jesus disorganizes the kingdom of darkness. It is for this reason that Satan will always throw tricks, and the 'system of doubt' to divert our attention from the power of Jesus to keep us in religious slavery! Believe in Jesus Christ, "I told you that you would die in your sins; if you do not believe that I am he, you will indeed die in your sins." **(John 8:24)** What is painful and alarming is that he who dies in his sins cannot inherit eternal life.

Some wonder what eternal life is. The answer is both simple and complex, "Now this is eternal life: that they know you, the only true God, and Jesus Christ, whom you have sent." **(John 17: 3)**

"We know also that the Son of God has come and has given us understanding, so that we may know him who is true. And we are in him who is true by being in his Son Jesus Christ. He is the true God and eternal life." **(1 John 5:20)**

Eternal life is only possible if we know **God** and whom He has sent; **Jesus Christ**. You cannot pretend to know and love God and disobey Him by rejecting his embodiment of salvation **JESUS CHRIST**.

What does Acts tell us? "Salvation is found in no one else, for there is no other name under heaven given to mankind by which we must be saved." **(Acts 4:12)**

Jesus has been given to us for our salvation. God gave Him to us. God's Word tells us that since the Old Testament, **Isaiah** the prophet received the revelation of the birth of the Messiah,

"Therefore the Lord himself will give you a sign: The virgin will conceive and give birth to a son, and will call him Immanuel." **(Isaiah 7:14)**

Has anyone ever seen a woman conceive without intercourse with a man? But Mary will give birth without intercourse for the holy child born of her came directly from heaven! Read **Matthew 1:18-23**, "This is how the birth of Jesus the Messiah came about: His mother Mary was pledged to be married to Joseph, but before they came together, she was found to be pregnant through the Holy Spirit. Because Joseph her husband was faithful to the law, and yet did not want to expose her to public disgrace, he had in mind to divorce her quietly. But after he had considered this, an angel of the Lord appeared to him in a dream and said, 'Joseph son of David, do not be afraid to take Mary home as your wife, because what is conceived in her is from the Holy Spirit. She will give birth to a son, and you are to give him the name Jesus, because he will save his people from their sins.' All this took place to fulfill what the Lord had said through the prophet: 'The virgin will conceive and give birth to a son, and they will call him Immanuel' (which means 'God with us')."

Jesus is the Word of God. He is the verb of God, and He is the Word made flesh. He is Emmanuel, God with us! Jesus Christ is God, descended to earth to establish the reign or kingdom of God in the heart of men. If we accept Him, we have accepted the kingdom of God. If we reject Him, we have rejected the kingdom of God, "Once, on being asked by the Pharisees when the kingdom of God would come, Jesus replied, '**The coming of the kingdom**

of God is not something that can be observed, nor will people say, 'Here it is,' or 'There it is,' **because the kingdom of God is in your midst.'"(Luke 17:20-21)**

Brothers and sisters, God's reign is already here on earth. On the day he arrived, the angels testified. Even those who have spoken in the heavens, "Therefore rejoice, you heavens and you who dwell in them! **But woe to the earth and the sea**, because the devil has gone down to you! He is filled with fury, because he knows that his time is short." **(Revelation 12:12)**

I will say it again, "Glory to God in the highest, and **on earth peace**, goodwill toward men." **(Luke 2:14 King James Version)**

Those who had previously said, "Woe to the earth" will repeat "Peace on the earth."

Why did the angels rejoice? What is this new announcement they came down to give? **"But the angel Said unto them [the shepherds] 'Fear not for behold, I bring you good tidings of great joy which shall be to all people. For unto you is born this day in the city of David a Savior, which is Christ the Lord." (Luke 2:9-11)**

Jesus Christ is the Savior, and He came down from heaven to establish peace on the earth! But beware, this peace is exclusively for men whom God has approved; those who have accepted His salvation plan! To accept Him is very simple. You must simply confess His name and declare what you feel deep in your heart, "If you declare with your mouth, 'Jesus is Lord,' and believe in your heart that God raised him from the dead, you will be saved. For it is with your heart that you believe and are justified, and it is with your mouth that you profess your faith and are saved. As Scripture says, 'Anyone who believes in him will never be put to shame.' For there is no difference between Jew and Gentile—the same Lord is Lord of all and richly blesses all who call on him, for, 'Everyone who calls on the name of the Lord will be saved.'" **(Romans 10:9-13)**

Before continuing, can you pray this prayer with me, "Lord Jesus, I accept You as my Lord and my Savior. I give You my life. Take my body, my soul and my mind. Forgive my sins and make me Your child. Support my faith so that I can be faithful to you all my life. Thank you Jesus for my name being written in the Book of Life! Amen."

Behold, you are saved through Him who gives life. Now that you have Jesus Christ, you can better understand the use of the His name in the spiritual warfare. But first, let's see some passages that prove that Jesus gives abundantly.

Jesus Gives Abundantly.
John 10:10- "I [Jesus] have come that they may have life and have it to the full"
3 John 2- "Dear friend, I pray that you may enjoy good health and that all may go well with you, even as your soul is getting along well."

Matthew 6:33- But seek first his kingdom and his righteousness, and all these things will be given to you as well."

When the Bible speaks of 'abundance' or 'all these things,' it's about good things that Christ came to give us.

"The blessing of the LORD brings wealth, without painful toil for it." **(Proverbs 10:22)**

Read this verse:

"For you know the grace of our Lord Jesus Christ, that though he was rich, yet for your sake he became poor, so that you through his poverty might become rich." **(2 Corinthians 8:9)**

Christ also came for our wealth, our abundance, and our prosperity. Is there a father who is against the financial prosperity of his offspring? Who wants his children to be the last in the society?

Who does not desire for people to speak well of their sons and daughters? Who does not want to live in the most beautiful houses, ride in luxury cars and be able to leave property for his descendants?

Who? Tell me! Every good parent is interested in the future of their children as children are an extension of their lives. Thus, God is interested in us, "'For I know the plans I have for you,' declares the LORD, 'plans to prosper you and not to harm you, plans to give you hope and a future.'" **(Jeremiah 29:11)**

This is similarly true for our God. God loves us and is willing to give all the good things we ask Him. His principle, His essence is to give. So we cannot and should not compare God to man, especially for the sharing of property to his children. **Matthew 7:9-11** tells us, "Which of you, if your son asks for bread, will give him a stone? Or if he asks for a fish, will give him a snake? If you, then, though you are evil, know how to give good gifts to your children, how much more will your Father in heaven give good gifts to those who ask him!"

God want us to prosper!

Paul said to the Philippians, "And my God will meet all your needs according to the riches of his glory in Christ Jesus." **(Philippians 4:19)** He has all things in His hands, **"With me are riches and honor, enduring wealth and prosperity." (Proverbs 8:18) "I walk in the way of righteousness, along the paths of justice, bestowing a rich inheritance on those who love me and making their treasuries full." (Proverbs 8:18, 20-21)**

But it benefits us to have the will to enter into this prophetic destiny that God has already given, "If you are willing and obedient, you will eat the good things of the land;" **(Isaiah 1:19)** Is it not what we see also in the book of Job, "What you decide on will be done, and light will shine on your ways." **(Job 22:28)**

Clearly, God wants us to enter heaven- His dwelling place- and be prosperous not only in heaven, but also from earth, "This is good, and pleases God our Savior, who wants all people to be saved and to come to a knowledge of the truth." **(1 Timothy 2:3-4)**

"And I [God] have promised to bring you up out of your misery in Egypt into the land of the Canaanites,

Hittites, Amorites, Perizzites, Hivites and Jebusites—a land flowing with milk and honey." **(Exodus 3:17)**

However, to arrive at these two designs of the Highest God, we must discern the power of the name of Jesus.

The Battle of Death!

There is a bitter water of truth that we must accept to be able to drink!

To enter into heaven is not all that easy!

There is a fierce battle to fight even if it cost us our lives! Jesus tells us,

"Whoever finds their life will lose it, and whoever loses their life for my sake will find it." **(Matthew 10:39)**

Here Jesus was not being an advocate for death, He Himself is life. Remember in the book of John, He brought Lazarus, a died man of four days, to life! It is, however, described that persecution will come to anyone willing to walk faithfully with Christ and they will suffer. If in the name of this persecution, some decided to renounce Christ to save their life, they shall lose because without Jesus, entering heaven is an impossibility. But if all the suffering because of the name of Jesus is endured and the persecution led to death, we would certainly lose our lives, but we find a sure path to heaven!

One thing is clear and certain, "Yea, and all that will live godly in Christ Jesus shall suffer persecution." **(2 Timothy 3:12)** This is why **Matthew 11:12** draws our attention, **"And from the days of John the Baptist until now the kingdom of heaven suffereth violence, and the violent take it by force."**

Will you accept to become violent to take possession of the kingdom of heaven? Who is he that the Bible calls the violent? It is he who accepts to remain faithful to Jesus despite what it may cost him. The violent who want to possess the Kingdom of God say, "I prefer that men uproot my life rather than renounce my faith in Christ and remain alive in the slavery of the devil to find myself in hell!"

For us, it is as Paul says, "Who shall separate us from the love of Christ? shall tribulation, or distress, or persecution, or famine, or nakedness, or peril, or sword? As it is written, For your sake we are killed all day long; we are accounted as sheep for the slaughter. Nay, in all these things we are more than conquerors through him who loved us. For I am persuaded that neither death, nor life, nor angels, nor principalities, nor powers, nor things present, nor things to come, nor height, nor depth, nor any other creature, shall be able to separate us from the love of God, which is in Christ Jesus our Lord." **(Romans 8:35-39)**

Behold the language of a violent people! Pragmatic people who know what they want! It is not a word they pronounce through the tip of the lips, but from the deep of the heart. It is not only seen in their best behavior, but also in their daily lives. Jesus Himself did not escape this spiritual warfare. Despite His divinity, He fought to be seated on the throne with His Father God, "To him that overcometh, will I grant to sit with Me in my throne, even as I also overcame, and am set down with My Father in His throne." **(Revelation 3:21)**

Jesus fought spiritually speaking. He faced the powers of darkness. At the Mount of Olives, Jesus fought in prayer so that His sweat became as drops of blood, "And being in agony, He [Jesus] prayed more earnestly, and **his sweat was like it were great drops of blood falling to the ground." (Luke 22:44)**

Christ fully accomplished his mission of salvation when He was hung on the cross of Calvary. It was at Golgotha that the mystery of salvation of the human race is found! Jesus saw death approaching and the agony of death seized him. He even prayed three times for it to be taken away from Him and at same time asked the will of His Father.

Matthew 26:38-39: "Then saith he unto them, My soul is exceeding sorrowful, even unto death: tarry ye here, and watch with me. And he went a little farther, and fell on his face, and prayed, saying, O my Father, if it be possible, let this cup pass from me: nevertheless not as I will, but as you will..."

"He went away again the second time and prayed saying, 'O my Father, if this cup may not pass away from me, except I drink it, your will be done.'"**(verse 42)**

"And he left them, and went away again, and prayed the third time, saying the same words." **(verse 44)**

The Cross

According to the plan of God, Jesus had to experience the crucifixion; it was decided by the Almighty! That is why God saw His will coming to pass as Jesus asked Him in His prayer. Spiritual warfare led Jesus to die on the venerated cross! The spiritual meaning of His death on the cross is very deep and one must be of the spirit to understand. This is why the Apostle Paul wrote these lines, "For the preaching of the cross is to them that perish foolishness, but unto us which are saved it is the power of God. For it is written: I will destroy the wisdom of the wise, and will bring to nothing the understanding of the prudent. Where is the wise? Where is the scribe? Where is the disputer of this world? Hath not God made the foolish the wisdom of this world? For after that in the wisdom of God the world by wisdom knew not God, it pleased God by the foolishness of preaching to save them that believe. Jews require a sign and the Greeks seek after wisdom: But we preach Christ crucified, unto the Jews a stumbling block and unto the Greek foolishness. But unto which are called, both Jews and Greeks, Christ the power of God and the wisdom of God. Because the foolishness of God is wiser than men, and the weakness of God is stronger than men." **(1 Corinthians 1:18-25)**

Let me tell you that God does not consider what we consider. God in His foreknowledge knew the importance of the cross in the salvation of the human being. His love for Jesus could not hinder from leading His Son to the cross! Jesus was to be condemned for us to be free. He had to die in order to give us life, so He was crucified, "And when they were come to the place, which is called the Calvary, they **Crucified him**, and the malefactors, one on the right hand, and the other on the left." **(Luke 23:33)**

"And he bearing his cross went forth into a place called the place of a skull, which is called in the Hebrew

Golgotha: Where they crucified him, and two other with him, on either side one, and Jesus in the midst. And Pilate wrote a title, and put it on the cross. And the writing was Jesus of Nazareth, the king of Jews. This title then read many of the Jews for the place where Jesus was crucified was nigh to the city: and it was written in Hebrew, Greek and Latin " **(John 19:17-20)**

The crucifixion was obviously a significant means of dying for God and therefore his Son, "When Jesus therefore had received the vinegar, he said, It is finished. And bowed his head, and gave up the ghost." **(John 19:30)** All these things happened according to plan and the verdict of God.

Indeed, it is on the cross that Jesus accomplished the work of redemption, deliverance, salvation, healing, success, elevation, and promotion. The secret of the victory lies in Golgotha where Jesus gave His life! In this warfare, the death of Jesus has become a gain for the children of God that we are! Hallelujah!

Our power, and our authority is found in the mystery of death that Christ experienced on the cross. This is where Satan was defeated, "Blotting out the handwriting of ordinances that was against us, which was contrary to us and took it out of the way, nailing it to the cross; having spoiled principalities and powers, he made a show of them openly, triumphing over them in it." **(Colossians 2:14-15)** It is through the cross of Jesus that we have victory, there He accomplished all. **(John 19:30)** This is why it's important for us as disciples to use this inevitable weapon- the name of Jesus- to cast out demons, "Behold,

I give unto you power to tread on serpents and scorpions, and over all the power of the enemy: and nothing shall by any means hurt you" **(Luke 10:19)**

Use the name of Jesus in spiritual warfare, "If ye shall ask any thing in my name, I will do it." **(John 14:14)** "And these signs shall follow them that believe; In my name shall they cast out devils; they shall speak with new tongues; They shall take up serpents; and if they drink any deadly thing, it shall not hurt them; they shall lay hands on the sick, and they shall recover." **(Mark 16: 17-18)** In short, in this battle, there is yet another mystery that is advantageous for the children of God that we are; the blood of Jesus that was shed. Thus, we have the second weapon that God used in spiritual warfare.

The Blood of Jesus

Calling on the Blood of Jesus, is to call on the total victory of God and His children on the devil and the angels followed him in his fall. Indeed, when Satan stood up against God in heaven, he was defeated by the Blood of the Lamb. **Revelation 12:11** reveals, **"And they (Michael and the Angels of God) overcame him by the blood of the Lamb..."**

For the earth to be delivered as it happened in heaven, it was necessary that blood be shed on earth as it had been in heaven. So Jesus came down from heaven to achieve on earth, the victory He had given to the inhabitants of heaven!

In spiritual warfare, we must never overlook the Blood of Jesus Christ. Remember that the blood has fought and defeated the devil and all the powers of darkness that rose up against us! In this blood, there is the power to shake the demons and even **dispossess** them of their power.

What happened when the death of Jesus was certified by the soldiers? **John 19:33-34** says, "But when they came to Jesus and found that he was already dead, they did not break his legs. 34 Instead, one of the soldiers pierced Jesus' side with a spear, bringing a sudden flow of blood and water."

Retain this very important lesson: whenever the Blood of Jesus touches the earth, it is deliverance. From the garden of Gethsemane to the cross, His blood was shed without measure. He was paying the penalty for our sins, **"For the life of a creature is in the blood**, and I have given it to you to make atonement for yourselves on the altar; **it is the blood that makes atonement for one's life."** **(Leviticus 17:11)** The blood plays an important role in the spiritual realm, however it must be recognized that blood has no power itself, but power is given to the blood by the person who is behind this blood. This person may be Satan or God! When we talk about the blood of Jesus, we speak of Almighty God that stands behind this blood. So God delivered us and saved us through the sacrifice of Christ and our faith.

Also, we have life through the Blood of Jesus that was shed for us. For the life of a man is in his blood. By giving His blood, Jesus was giving His life as a substitute for the penalty of our sins that would lead to death. He took our death and gave us life through His blood. His death saved our souls and gave us life.

The blood of bulls and goats from **Hebrews 10:4** could not take away sins. In fact, there is no power in the blood as a substance, but the power is in covenant represented by the blood. You understand therefore that the blood of animals was a symbol; a shadow of what was to happen in the New Testament. The old covenant with the blood of bulls and goats was insufficient, it needed a new covenant! That is why Christ said, "Wherefore when he cometh into the world, he saith, Sacrifice and offering you would not, but you have prepared a body for me: In burnt offerings and sacrifices for sin you have had no pleasure. Then said I, Lo, I come… to do your will, O God." **(Hebrews 10:5-7)** Christ is indeed the perfect will of God. And it is through Him that the new covenant was established of course through His blood!

Meditate on **Hebrews 8:7-8**, "For if there had been nothing wrong with that first covenant, no place would have been sought for another. But God found fault with the people and said: 'The days are coming, declares the Lord, when I will make a new covenant with the people of Israel and with the people of Judah.'". Here we see clearly that in the first covenant, there were defects which brought about the need for a new covenant woven by the Blood of Jesus!

Whosoever rejects the covenant represented by the blood refuses a powerful weapon that God gave him and attracts a judgment and punishment against himself, "How much more severely do you think someone deserves to be punished who has trampled the Son of God underfoot, who has treated as an unholy thing the blood of the covenant that sanctified them, and who has insulted the Spirit of grace? For we know him who said, 'It is mine to avenge; I will repay,' and again, 'The Lord will judge his people.' It is a dreadful thing to fall into the hands of the living God." **(Heb. 10:29-31)**

Accepting that the Blood of Christ was shed for us, we accept God who stands behind this blood. And by refusing, we refuse God who is always behind the blood! The secret is that God gives us His power and His authority because henceforth our sins are now forgiven because of the blood of Jesus. Once we accept Jesus, we are forgiven and God gives us authority! So we can say to a demon or an unclean spirit or Satan himself, "They triumphed over him by the blood of the Lamb and by the word of their testimony; they did not love their lives so much as to shrink from death." **(Revelation 12:11)** just to remind him of his defeat.

However, in spiritual warfare, we do not cast out a demon by the Blood of Jesus, we must overcome by the blood of Jesus and we cast them out by the Name of Jesus. Two references offer a better understanding of this, "They overcame him Blood of the Lamb..." **(Revelation 12:11)** and, "In my name they will drive out demons..." **(Mark 16:17)**

We can pray in this way:

"Satan, you are defeated because of the Blood of Jesus, I declare your failure in my life and I cast you out in the name of Jesus!"

It is advantageous to accept that the blood of Jesus was shed for us. Simply enter the new covenant because the consequences are positive and plentiful: let us see a few. By His blood,

We have redemption, forgiveness **(Ephesians 1:7)** Indeed, all the descendants of Adam were sold, we were all slaves of the devil and were therefore under his domination because of sin. To be redeemed from death, the wages of sin, **(Romans 6: 23a)** Jesus paid our debt by dying and took our place by shedding His blood! We can no longer be in prison or slaves because Jesus gave His life for us. He has redeemed us by destroying he that has the power of death; that is the devil. We are therefore free from any kind of bondage. **(Hebrews 2:14-15)**

Meditate on **Hebrews 9:12,** "He did not enter by means of the blood of goats and calves; but he entered the Most Holy Place once for all by his own blood, thus obtaining eternal redemption."

"In fact, the law requires that nearly everything be cleansed with blood, and without the shedding of blood there is no forgiveness." **(Hebrews 9:22)**

We are justified, "Since we have now been justified by his blood, how much more shall we be saved from God's wrath through him!" **(Romans 5:9)** Every sinner who believes in Jesus and confesses Him becomes righteous before God because God does not see him, but He sees His Son Jesus through the converted sinner, "God made him who had no sin to be sin for us, so that in him we might become the righteousness of God." **(2 Corinthians 5:21)**

We are cleansed, as long as we walked in the light and we keep the fellowship. "But if we walk in the light, as he is in the light, we have fellowship with one another, and the blood of Jesus, his Son, purifies us from all sin." **(1 John 1:7)** The Blood of Jesus continues to cleanse us even as Christians if we happen to sin against God, "If we claim to be without sin, we deceive ourselves and the truth is not in us. If we confess our sins, he is faithful and just and will forgive us our sins and purify us from all unrighteousness." **(verses 8-9)**

We are sanctified. "And so Jesus also suffered outside the city gate to make the people holy through his own blood." **(Hebrews 13:12)** To be sanctified is to be set aside as the private property of God. He does not want to share us with Satan for any reason at all. A new road was opened to lead us into the presence of God, "Therefore, brothers and sisters, since we have confidence to enter the Most Holy Place by the blood of Jesus, by a new and living way opened for us through the curtain, that is, his body," **(Hebrews 10:19-20)** In the Old Testament, the sanctuary was divided into three parties. The people stayed at the court and the priests in the holy place, and only the high priest had the right to enter the most holy place protected by a veil. It is this veil that Jesus tore through his death to enable us to enter without exclusion into the presence of God. The flesh of Jesus was torn and His blood shed. It is finished. There is no more veil; we can all enter into the most holy place without running the risk of dying!

We are answered because His blood intercedes for us, "to Jesus the mediator of a new covenant, and to the sprinkled blood that speaks a better word than the blood of Abel." **(Hebrews 12:24)**

When we pray for a subject, Jesus intervenes and reminds God to remember His blood was shed for us. When it comes to us to fall accidentally into any sin and we ask for forgiveness from God, the blood of Jesus speaks for us. Here, it is to be recalled that the Blood of Jesus is far different from any human blood. In fact, what men do not know is that each time they shed the blood of another human being in whatever manner or form, once the blood touches the land, he asks vengeance as the blood of Abel asked when his brother Cain killed him. **(Genesis 4:8, 10)** The Blood of Jesus implores God's forgiveness for us in these and all matters! However, do not invoke the Blood of Jesus as a person to replace God. No, it is simply a weapon to be used. When it is invoked, only the Lord should be invoked. **(Psalm 50:15, Romans 10:12-13 & Revelation 12:11)**

We have eternal life, "Whoever eats my flesh and drinks my blood has eternal life, and I will raise them up at the last day." **(John 6:54)** The list of what the Blood of Jesus brings to us is too long to be written. This is what the devil does not like about spiritual warfare. He tries to keep us in the Old Testament where they sacrificed animals. There is no blood that is as pure as the blood of Jesus, son of God, conceived by the power of the Holy Spirit. The deceiver knows this and seeks to blind the eyes of the faithful.

Enter the new covenant through the Blood of Jesus! What does **Hebrews 8:13** tell us, "By calling this covenant 'new,' he has made the first one obsolete; and what is obsolete and outdated will soon disappear."

Why do you cling to what is old? Especially the old things God has seen fit to replace with a new thing. Jesus came from God. He gave himself on the cross for us, so there is no sacrifice to do again. The History told us that war of posters or billboard at 16th century, **MARCOURTS** posted a furious lampoon. On page 44 of "Literature Life Under Rebirth" by Auguste Bailly it is stated, **"The sacrifice of Jesus Christ was perfect and should never be repeated by any visible sacrifice."** It is the truth. For every sacrifice made outside of the Blood of Jesus, we grow dedication to the demons as it is approved by the devil. The Apostle Paul did not say otherwise in **1 Corinthians 10:20, "No, but the sacrifices of pagans are offered to demons, not to God, and I do not want you to be participants with demons."**

In short, know that demons are already defeated by the Blood of Jesus. Cast them out in the name of Jesus and you will see the result. In addition, three days after His crucifixion, Jesus came out alive from the tomb and spent some time on earth. However, before ascending to heaven, he made the promise of another powerful weapon; The Holy Spirit.

<u>The Holy Spirit</u>

When we speak of the Holy Spirit in spiritual warfare as a weapon, you must understand that it is God Himself who has invested this powerful weapon in us. This is the reference:

John 4:24: "God is Spirit "

Malachi 3:6: "I the LORD do not change."

Psalm 82:6: "I said, 'You are 'gods'; you are all sons of the Most High.'"

John 3:8: "The wind blows wherever it pleases. You hear its sound, but you cannot tell where it comes from or where it is going. So it is with everyone born of the Spirit."

Indeed if God is a Spirit who does not change- because in Him there is neither shadow of change- and this God lives in us, then we become invincible!

But the question becomes: How do we reach this level? How can we be in the fullness of Spirit and fight spirits with the help of the Holy Spirit?

The answer is very simple for those who want to follow the plan and the will of God in spiritual warfare. Do we not say that our God is a God of order? An omniscient God?

Since the Old Testament, He promised the arrival of His Spirit on earth through the prophet **Joel (2:28)**, "And afterward, **I will pour out my Spirit on all people...**" The great prophet Ezekiel also received the same message, "I will give you a new heart and put a new spirit in you; I will remove from you your heart of stone and give you a heart of flesh. 27 And **I will put my Spirit in you** and move you to follow my decrees and be careful to keep my laws." **(Ezekiel 36:26-27)** God decided to spread His Spirit in the last days for it will be difficult times. **(1 Timothy 3:1-7)**

For us to get to the stage of the perfect will of God, imperatively we must have God Himself in our lives through His Spirit. I think the apostle Paul understood this; when our bodies lead us in mortal things and when we are as dead spiritually as Adam and Eve, we need the Spirit of Him who raised Jesus from the dead, "And if the Spirit of him who raised Jesus from the dead is living in you, he who raised Christ from the dead will also give life to your mortal bodies because of his Spirit who lives in you." **(Romans 8:11)** And if we have His Spirit, we can no longer practice the works of the devil. As we are overcoming in the spiritual, we become a poison to the enemy.

Paul continues in verses **12-16**, "Therefore, brothers and sisters, we have an obligation—but it is not to the flesh, to live according to it. For if you live according to the flesh, you will die; but if by the Spirit you put to death the misdeeds of the body, you will live. For those who are led by the Spirit of God are the children of God. The Spirit you received does not make you slaves, so that you live in fear again; rather, the Spirit you received brought about your adoption to sonship. And by him we cry, 'Abba, Father.' The Spirit himself testifies with our spirit that we are God's children."

Who would dare touch someone under the shelter of the Most High? The Holy Spirit will fight him! The apostle tells us in **verse 31, "If God is for us, who can be against us?"** Who can venture to attack the most powerful country in arms if he himself is not sure of the power of weapons he possesses?

If we are with God, and He is in us by His Spirit, it must be explicitly understood that our enemies can never defeat us! The Holy Spirit will reveal and chase him. **Isaiah 59:19** explains, "So shall they fear the name of the LORD from the west, and his glory from the rising of the sun. When the enemy shall come in like a flood, the Spirit of the LORD shall lift up a standard against him."

Let me tell you that to receive the Holy Spirit and His fullness- to be victorious- we must have Jesus in our lives.

It is for this reason that He Himself reiterated the same promise to His disciples and asked them to wait in Jerusalem. One cannot witness the power of God without being coated by the Spirit of God,

"On one occasion, while he was eating with them, he gave them this command: 'Do not leave Jerusalem, but wait for the gift my Father promised, which you have heard me speak about. For John baptized with water, but in a few days you will be baptized with the Holy Spirit.' But you will receive power when the Holy Spirit comes on you; and you will be my witnesses in Jerusalem, and in all Judea and Samaria, and to the ends of the earth." (Acts 1:4-5, 8)

Jesus knew that He had fulfilled His mission on the cross but going without equipping His disciples with the power of the Holy Spirit would be a big error! For Satan is here as prince of this world, and we should not ignore that he is ingenious in evil. To prevent this, the Master promised His disciples that He would not leave them as orphans, but He sent another Comforter which is the Holy Spirit. Note here, that the devil has, through his strategy, deceived thousands of people who now believe the promise of another Comforter was a human being. Big mistake! What does the Scripture say? "And I will ask the Father, and he will give you **another advocate to help you and be with you forever**— the Spirit of truth. The world cannot accept him, because it neither sees him nor knows him. But you know him, **for he lives with you and will be in you.** I will not leave you as orphans; I will come to you." **(John 14:16-18)**

We must recognize that Jesus did not speak of a visible man but of the Holy Spirit which is invisible. There are sizes of details that should not be ignored in this:

"Let [the Comforter] be with you forever"

"The Spirit of truth, which the world cannot receive, because it seeth him not and knoweth him not."

That which we do not see and is eternal because He came from God can only be the Spirit. Jesus was talking about the Holy Spirit in these verses.

It is a tortuous weapon against the enemy in the spiritual battle! That is why the devil uses all his energy to distract children of God from this weapon that was given to them.

However, this promise was fulfilled on the day of Pentecost, according to the promise of God and the command given by Jesus to His disciples. Do you see that there is a logical sequence in all these events? **Acts 2** tells us the story of the descent of the Holy Spirit,

"When the day of Pentecost came, they were all together in one place. Suddenly a sound like the blowing of a violent wind came from heaven and filled the whole house where they were sitting. They saw what seemed to be tongues of fire that separated and came to rest on each of them. All of them were filled with the Holy Spirit and began to speak in other tongues as the Spirit enabled them." **(Acts 2:1-4)**

Praying in tongues or in the spirit, sends fire into the camp of the enemy. When the Bible speaks of language similar to the 'tongues of fire', it is the power of Most High God, a consuming fire, that we are showing! This is why he who prays in the spirit is not talking to men but to God, who executes His wrath upon the wicked spirit that stresses us. Read the Word of God, **"For anyone who speaks in a tongue does not speak to people but to God. Indeed, no one understands them; they utter mysteries by the Spirit." (1 Corinthians 14:2)**

When we say mysteries in the battles made in the spirit realm and by the Spirit, the God that understands mysteries comes down and acts in our favor. What does **2 Thessalonians 1:6** say? **"God is just: He will pay back trouble to those who trouble you"** The only problems are our obedience to God and our familiarity with the weapons He has given us is not yet complete, "And we will be ready to punish every act of disobedience, once your obedience is complete." **(2 Corinthians 10:6)**

Everyone needs the Holy Spirit. In all cases, everybody who wants to win and sit on the throne with God and enjoy a good life on earth, should be fighting with this weapon. The promise is also for them. Indeed, when the disciples spoke in other tongues or rather said mysteries through the tongues of fire that they received, their contemporaries were present but amazed! Some even thought they had become drunk from wine. By this even Peter, who had lost the battle three times denying the Lord, would win this time because he was armed with the Holy Spirit. He would, moreover, explain the Word of God and His promise from the Old Testament to its fulfillment in the New Testament. But the most interesting is that he makes them understand like us today, **"The promise is for you and your children and for all who are far off — for all whom the Lord our God will call." (Acts 2:39)**

The promise is for all children of God. Jesus Himself needed the Holy Spirit in His earthly ministry. He always worked with the help of the Holy Spirit. And we too must if we really want to win over the witches, warlocks, and powers of darkness that oppose the purpose of God for the salvation of the children of God; our happiness and blessings. On the day of His baptism in the Jordan, the Spirit descended upon Him, "When all the people were being baptized, **Jesus was baptized too. And as he was praying, heaven was opened and the Holy Spirit descended on him in bodily form like a dove.** And a voice came from heaven: 'You are my Son, whom I love; with you I am well pleased.'" **(Luke 3:21-22)**

Without the power of the Holy Spirit, nobody, whatever their intellectual strength, can resist the devil. **Job 32:8** says, "But it is the spirit in a person, the breath of the Almighty, that gives them understanding." The breath of God must meet with our spirit so that it can come back to life in order to face the devil!

Isn't that what God tells us in **Ezekiel 37:9-10**?

"Then he said to me, 'Prophesy to the breath; prophesy, son of man, and say to it, 'This is what the Sovereign LORD says: Come, breath, from the four winds and breathe into these slain, that they may live.'' So I prophesied as he commanded me, and breath entered them; they came to life and stood up on their feet—a vast army."

We can stand up and form a large army if and only if the Lord of hosts, equips us with His Spirit, (that is to say that the wind of the Great Spirit with capital letter 'S' touch the small spirit with small letter 's' that we are.) Then the victory is assured.

To face with the devil, Jesus used this weapon. It is a must! Luke tells us very clearly, "Jesus, full of the Holy Spirit, left the Jordan and was led by the Spirit into the wilderness, where for forty days he was tempted by the devil. He ate nothing during those days, and at the end of them he was hungry." **(Luke 4:1-2)**

Think about Samson and the lion in the book of **Judges 14:6**, the Bible says, "The Spirit of the LORD came powerfully upon him so that he tore the lion apart with his bare hands as he might have torn a young goat. But he told neither his father nor his mother what he had done."

It is the Spirit! God works through us to have victory over all opposition. I understand why the disciples could not do anything other than wait for His arrival. The Scriptures call Him:

The Holy Spirit (1 Thessalonians 4:8)

The Spirit of God (Ephesians 4:30; Genesis 1:2, 1 Corinthians 2:11)

The Spirit of Christ (Rom. 8:9)

The Comforter (John 15:28)

Retain a very important lesson:

It is God who gives or rather sends his Spirit, "But the Advocate, the Holy Spirit, whom the Father will send in my name, will teach you all things and will remind you of everything I have said to you." **(John 14:26)** But beware, through His Son that He will spread on us, "Exalted to the right hand of God, he has received from the Father the promised Holy Spirit and has poured out what you now see and hear." **(Acts 2:33)**

This thought may be clearer in our minds if we read **John 14:18-20**, "I will not leave you as orphans; I will come to you. Before long, the world will not see me anymore, but you will see me. Because I live, you also will live. On that day you will realize that I am in my Father, and you are in me, and I am in you." Jesus works in us by His Spirit! This is the truth!

See also **1 John 4:4** saying, "You, dear children, are from God and have overcome them, because the one who is in you is greater than the one who is in the world." He lives in us and makes the impossible possible!

The Impossible Becomes Possible

This is undoubtedly the revelation that Mary, the mother of Jesus, received from the angel who was sent to her when angel Gabriel told her the promises of God, "You will conceive, and bear a Son, and you will call his name Jesus. He will be great and will be called Son of God Most High, and the Lord God will give Him the throne of David, His Father. He will reign over the house of Jacob forever, and His kingdom will never end." She opened her eyes wide because for her it was impossible! And without a doubt she was right because humanly speaking, it takes sexual intercourse for a woman to conceive. We know Mary's reaction, "How can this be, since I know not man?"

Like Mary, we also ask ourselves countless questions in spiritual warfare. One wonders how will this be, how will it be possible? Can the promises that God made to me be realized? Can I really win, get married, prosper, succeed, or travel considering I have neither this nor that, and no one help me!

I'm here to reassure you. Listen to the answer given by the angel to Mary. God is giving you the same answer so that the impossible becomes possible, **"The Holy Ghost shall come upon you, and the power of the Most High shall overshadow you."**

Yes, the Holy Spirit will come upon you, break the yoke. The Holy Spirit will set you free so you can possess your possessions and your inheritance!

Isaiah 10:27 said, "In that day their burden will be lifted from your shoulders, their yoke from your neck; the yoke will be broken because you have grown so fat." Whatever the internal (nightmares, bad dreams, white night...) or external warfare that we are going through, the Spirit of God is ready to help us. Yes, we have a treasure in an earthen vessel! **(2 Corinthians 4:7)**

Do you want your yoke to explode? Do you want to preach with boldness? Seek for the Holy Spirit, using Him in spiritual warfare and praying sometimes in tongues, **(1 Corinthians 14:18)** you will see the results and you will give testimony. However, receiving the Spirit is not enough; we must continue to pursue the goals and the purposes and plans of God, to save all men by means of preaching. **(1Timothy 2: 4-6)**

What did God tell Zerubbabel in **Zechariah 4:6** concerning the mountain that stood before him? "'Not by might nor by power, but by my Spirit,' says the LORD Almighty." This mountain must move. Amen! However, we must recognize that for the Spirit to work, and for one to get results, the weapon of the word should not to be neglected.

The Word of God

The word in spiritual warfare as a weapon has an inestimable value before God. In fact, it is spirit and life according to **John 6:63;** hence the need to know how to use and manipulate it in your favor! It is a double-edged sword that requires delicacy in the way it is used! To better convey the revelation of the Spirit, we will start from the Word of God to reach our own words and finish with our mind which is the dumbed word.

The Word of God

Let's start with an undeniable truth: God and His word are one; "In the beginning God..." also, "In the beginning was the word..." **(Genesis 1:1, John 1:1)** This means that the word was existing well before the creation and it has not been made material to us! For a miracle to happen, the word must go first! This is what the book of **Genesis** tells us! Certainly, the Spirit was there and moved upon the water, but darkness also was there and covered the surface of the abyss! Light emerged only when God spoke, "Now the earth was formless and empty, darkness was over the surface of the deep, and the Spirit of God was hovering over the waters. And God said, "Let there be light," and there was light." **(Chapter 1:2-3)**

The miracle of light occurred because God spoke.

What happened? There were complementary functions between the Spirit and the Word of God. Indeed, when the weapon of the Word was used, a connection was produced- a symbiosis, an osmosis, or rather a mixture- a fusion between this weapon and the weapon that is the spirit. It was then that the result of light was obtained. To see the light of God illuminate the darkness of your life, you must fight quoting the Word of God! It is by His word that God created the heavens and the earth, sea, different waters, forests, savannahs, and animals.

The word that comes from the mouth of God always produces a result because when God speaks, it happens! "As the rain and the snow come down from heaven, and do not return to it without watering the earth and making it bud and flourish, so that it yields seed for the sower and bread for the eater, *11* so is my word that goes out from my mouth: It will not return to me empty, but will accomplish what I desire and achieve the purpose for which I sent it." **(Isaiah 55:10-11)** What was the will of God, what was His purpose when creating man? The Bible answers, "Then God said, "Let us make mankind in our image, in our likeness, so that they may rule over the fish in the sea and the birds in the sky, over the livestock and all the wild animals, and over all the creatures that move along the ground." **(Genesis 1:26)**

The Word of God is irrevocable, it does not return to Him without obtaining the result that God expects! Somewhere you can be successful in your life! There is a part of the earth where you have to dominate! You cannot fail or die without having dominion over the portion of earth that your God had given you. While in warfare, you can lose the battle but not the war. Rise up and continue the battle. "Consider how far you have fallen!" **(Revelation 2:5)**

Note your misstep and mark very well the place in order not to fall again and continue the battle until you're sure you've dominated the Earth. It is not in vain that God gave the power to speak to man! Remember that the first job- the first activity man had after his creation- was to 'speak.' It is through the word that man began his work on earth. Read with me **Genesis 2:19-20**, "Now the LORD God had formed out of the ground all the wild animals and all the birds in the sky. He brought them to the man to see what he would name them; and whatever the man called each living creature, that was its name. So the man gave names to all the livestock, the birds in the sky and all the wild animals. But for Adam no suitable helper was found."

It is undoubtedly for this reason that the Psalmist exclaimed, "I said, 'You are 'gods'; you are all sons of the Most High.'" **(Psalm 82:6)** God has given us everything, "You made them rulers over the works of your hands; you put everything under their feet:" **(Psalm 8:6)**

However, for all the authority that God gave to man, he was not able to protect himself and the devil robbed him by leading him to sin. God in His love can in no way throw in the towel by abandoning man in his situation. So He would send the master of the word to fight the devil where man has failed! So, God sends an angel to Mary, the angel will have pronounced 'the Word of God' and this word was made flesh, "In the beginning was the Word, and the Word was with God, and the Word was God. He was with God in the beginning" **(John 1:1-2)** "The Word became flesh and made his dwelling among us. We have seen his glory, the glory of the one and only Son, who came from the Father, full of grace and truth." **(John 1:14)**

One can say that God came down to earth, for His word must be fulfilled at all cost in the life of man. His children are to be revealed in the creation by their reign, their domination. This had been revealed to the prophet Isaiah, "Therefore the Lord himself will give you a sign: The virgin will conceive and give birth to a son, and will call him Immanuel." **(Isaiah 7:14)** has found its fulfillment in the New Testament in **Matthew 1:23.** It is here that we find the meaning of the name 'Emmanuel' meaning, "... God with us."

Let me tell you that Jesus is the Word of God and the word with us. As Jesus is with us, it is God Himself who is with us! You cannot separate a man from his voice! Remember that God is in His Word, He surrounds His word, and He watches over His word for its fulfillment. When He sent Moses to Egypt to deliver Israel from slavery, He had given His word to Moses. Unfortunately, men could not grasp the meaning of this revelation, "God said to Moses, "I AM WHO I AM. This is what you are to say to the Israelites: 'I AM has sent me to you.'" **(Exodus 3:14)**

Repetition is teaching, God will renew His word through His son Jesus, who will explain in greater detail, what is the mystery of, "I am that I am." In fact, John, who was always beside the Master, took the time to teach us these words in the Gospel that bears his name, "I am that I am" has come down from heaven to reveal who He is.

Listen to him:
- "I am the bread of life" **(John 6:35)**
- "I am the light of the world" **(Chapter 8:12)**
- "I am the door" **(Chapter 10:9)**
- "I am the good shepherd" **(Chapter 10:11)**
- "I am the resurrection and the life" **(Chapter 11:25)**
- "I am the true vine" **(Chapter 15:1)**
- "I am the way, the truth and the life" **(Chapter 14:6)**

Despite this revelation, Satan, the enemy of God, was not afraid and saw in Jesus the one who has conquered the heaven, "They triumphed over him by the blood of the Lamb and by the word of their testimony…" **(Revelation 12:11)** And Satan will trigger another battle against Him for the Lamb spoken of here is indeed Jesus, the Word made flesh, whom we bear witness. Jean-Baptist was right when he said,

"Look, the Lamb of God, who takes away the sin of the world!" **(John 1:29)** This is Jesus, the Lamb of God who destroys the devil's plan in heaven. When He came down to earth, Satan recognized Him and engaged in another battle.

Retain a lesson: Satan does not give up easily. That is why the Scripture implores us to resist him and he will eventually flee. **(James 4:7)** If we do not resist him, he will eventually have us as he had to Adam and Eve. Jesus resisted him, but by the Word of God which is a very effective weapon. In the fourth chapter of Matthew, we saw how the tempter came to Jesus.

Indeed, Jesus had just finished forty days fasting, and the crafty enemy, knowing the immediate need for a man who has just finished fasting, will offer him something that is not impossible, but is not useful, "The tempter came to him and said, 'If you are the Son of God, tell these stones to become bread.'" **(Matthew 4:3)** Jesus understood that the devil came to tempt Him. Do not forget his 'system of doubt' with which he was able to lead Adam and Eve to their fall, "Did God really say?…" He will use the same system, "If you are a son of God," God had actually told

Adam and Eve not to eat the forbidden fruit, and Jesus is truly the Son of God! Satan uses the truth he knows to make children of God doubt in regard to the word and the promise of their Father.

We have to resist him through the Word of God by following the example of our master Jesus Christ. "Jesus answered, "It is written: 'Man shall not live on bread alone, but on every word that comes from the mouth of God.'" **(Matthew 4:4)** Jesus used the weapon- the Word- to defeat the devil and he was able to quote scripture because he knew the Word. He did not ignore the word of His Father as was the case of the elder brother in the parable of the prodigal son who **asked a servant what was happening in the house of his own Father. (Luke 15:26)**

Ignorance is slavery. We need to know the Word of God, meditating day and night. **(Joshua 1:8)**

What happened in Eden in the garden is very painful. Adam and Eve were created in the image and likeness of God and did not need to listen to the lies of the devil that made them believe they would be as gods; knowing good and evil. They were already small gods!

But glory be to God in the Heaven for if the first Adam failed, the second won the victory! Amen!

If Satan tried to touch your body and did not succeed, he will try to take your soul! The bread is made to nourish the body and many people fall in this first degree of spiritual warfare. The second degree is situated at the level of the soul, where the headquarters of passion is located. Do philosophers not say that nothing great on earth is done without passion? Thus Satan will tell Jesus to cast himself down from the temple.

It was the soul of Jesus that was targeted by the devil in the second degree of combat. And here, Satan would go further because he would also quote a verse of the Bible to convince Jesus, "If you are the Son of God," he said, "throw yourself down. For it is written: 'He will command his angels concerning you, and they will lift you up in their hands, so that you will not strike your foot against a stone.'" **(Matthew 4:6)**

It is the time to remind the children of God, that we should be specialists in the Word of God for our enemy- the accuser- does not ignore the word of the Almighty God. He knows more and thusly will deform the Word in his favor by quoting verses halfway or out of their context. One must then be a specialist in the field like our master, "Jesus answered him, 'It is also written: 'Do not put the Lord your God to the test.''" **(Matthew 4:7)** What will Jesus gain by jumping from such a place? Wherein would God be glorified if he did it? There are things that men will attempt to make us do under the influence of demons. Reject them because we know that our God will not be glorified in our doing it! Say it like Paul, "'I have the right to do anything,' you say—but not everything is beneficial. 'I have the right to do anything' — but I will not be mastered by anything." **(1 Corinthians 6:12)**

Let us not be enslaved by anything, even if there are verses quoted out of context.

Having failed once again, Satan would rise to the third degree of spiritual warfare by presenting the glory of this world to Jesus. It is at this level that politicians, authorities, and some "servants of God "-those who are thirsty for worldly things- depart to worship Lucifer the devil, to meet with him in the fire, after their life on earth.

What part of us do we use to worship either God or Satan? Our spirit is the place of worship. **(John 4:24)** The spirit of Jesus was attacked by the devil, "Again, the devil took him to a very high mountain and showed him all the kingdoms of the world and their splendor. 9 'All this I will give you,' he said, '**If you will bow down and worship me.**'" **(Matthew 4:8-9)**

Let this demonstrated point be clearly stated:

The response of Jesus to these three levels of battle is always based on the Word of God, "Jesus said to him, 'Away from me, Satan! For it is written: 'Worship the Lord your God, and serve him only.'" **(Matthew 4:10)**

It is necessary to know that spiritual warfare is growing.

The more you seek God, and the more you fast, the more the devil will send great trials. If you resist, at a given time you take authority and the demons are obliged to leave. Jesus added a word of authority to the Word of God, "Get you hence, Satan!" **Verse 11** says, "Then the devil left him, and angels came and attended him." There is a spiritual level you have to reach for the battles to end between you and Satan! Not that he will not come back- he will come back to attack you one way or another- but you should take authority, and he will obey. We see this in the book of Acts, where a woman possessed by a spirit of python bored Paul and Silas. The Bible says, "Finally Paul became so annoyed that he turned around and said to the spirit, "In the name of Jesus Christ I command you to come out of her!" At that moment the spirit left her." **(Acts 16:18)**

Spiritual warfare is real and serious. Satan attacks every day, he always tries to exercise his devouring ministry "Be alert and of sober mind. Your enemy the devil prowls around like a roaring lion looking for someone to devour." **(1 Peter 5:8)**

If Jesus overcame Satan by the Word of God, we can do the same! What I remember from this battle is that the devil came to test the Word of God by the Word of God. The Word of God defeated him by the Word of God! Amen!

If we are small, Christ and the Word of God dwells largely in us, we will always win.

Here are a few advantages to listening, meditating, and studying the Word of God **(2 Timothy 3:16; Exodus 31:18)**

When we pray, we are talking to God. But when it comes to reading, listening, or studying the Word of God, we are allowing God to speak to us. And while he speaks to us, since He Himself is the Word, He is investing in us.

Then the resulting benefits are extraordinary, let cite some examples:

It gives us the faith **(Romans 10:1)**

It leads to success and good success **(Joshua 1:8)**

It makes wise, intelligent, it educates **(Psalms 119: 98-100, 104)**

It keeps us far from every evil way **(Psalms 119:101)**

It is the light that shines on us **(Psalms 119:105; John 8:12)**

It heals all our diseases **(Psalms 107:20; Isaiah 53:5)**

It delivers from all evil spirits **(Matthew 8:16)**

Through it, we overcome all as by the blood **(Revelation 12:11)**

Through it, we receive the Holy Spirit promised by God. **(Acts 10:44-46)**

By it we receive unto salvation **(Romans 10:13-15)**

It gives us the power to become children of God **(John 1:12)**

The Lord Jesus Christ lives in us through His word **(Galatians 2:20)**

It makes us bold as citizens of heaven on the earth. And all our thoughts and our interests are fixed on the things above. The example Stephen will edify us **(Acts 7:55, 59-60)**

We must therefore hear the word so that our spirit can be connected with God who communicates His spirit to us

From these passages, you understand that the Word of God can never cease to be proclaimed:

"Heaven and earth will pass away, but my words will never pass away." **(Luke 21:33)**

"Lift up your eyes to the heavens, look at the earth beneath; the heavens will vanish like smoke, the earth will wear out like a garment and its inhabitants die like flies. But my salvation will last forever, my righteousness will never fail." **(Isaiah 51:6)**

But God has a 'problem'! His desire and His will is that "[He] wants all people to be saved and to come to a knowledge of the truth." **(1 Timothy 2:4)** But He cannot preach Himself! It is not in vain that scripture says that God is seeking for a man **(Ezekiel 22:30)** and did not find! God needs men to proclaim His Word which leads other people to change so he does not destroy the country, the land or the nation.

The harvest is great, and I do not believe there are few workers. There are many workers (we see them today) but only a few are faithful. **(Luke 10:2)**

Is this not the reason The Bible tells us that many are called, but few are chosen!

Where do you stand, servant of God?

Are you among the called or are you among the chosen?

People of God in Spiritual Warfare

We are obliged to make a bridge to speak on the heart of God to His servants. I was in a moment of fasting and prayer and God gave me a dream, "We were many, in a very big hall. All, without exception, were dressed in beautiful clothes waiting for the one who called the meeting to talk to us, men and women of God. Sometime later, I saw an old man, yes an old man! A man well advanced in age! All his hair, his eyelashes and eyebrows were white, but he had the strength of a young man. He walked straight in his white robe and stopped on the platform. Immediately, all the men of God who were greeting themselves, embracing themselves kept quiet and stared at him! We had no choice. His word and his voice filled the hall and my soul was wounded inside of me! 'Among you, as many as you are, he that is sure that he is faithful and he preaches exclusively my word, he should come up here to me. You have forgotten my word, your greatest wish is to fill your pockets by talking about yourself, the value of your outfits forgetting to proclaim CHRIST. Reuben slept with the wife of his father. He stole the place that belonged to his father, he was not blessed. I am waiting, come up,' he said. Radio silence! Heads were bowed down; I lifted my head to see if there was anyone who would take a step towards him... Nobody! And the old man continued, 'It will be better if you pay the price because you were called and to preach the true gospel.'"

Take note and read: **2 Corinthians 4:5 & Mark 10:29-31**!

I can hear the old man saying, "Understand one thing; no one can work for me and die without having received the reward of his work!"

Which government does not pay its legislators? Which country will refuse to support its ambassadors? Preach my word faithfully and you will see! "Then the old man pointed his finger at me and said, 'Write these things that you have seen and heard. I give you the task and responsibility of the message so that it does not pass over in silence!'

When I woke up, it was three o'clock in the morning. My eyes were really wet with tears and I was without strength, confused thinking about what I had just seen and heard. Moments later, I took my Bible to read the verses he had given as they were still fresh in my mind, "For what we preach is not ourselves, but Jesus Christ as Lord, and ourselves as your servants for Jesus' sake." **(2 Corinthians 4:5)**

And Jesus answered and said, "'Truly I tell you,' Jesus replied, 'none who has left home or brothers or sisters or mother or father or children or fields for me and the gospel will fail to receive a hundred times as much in this present age: homes, brothers, sisters, mothers, children and fields—along with persecutions—and in the age to come eternal life. But many who are first will be last, and the last first.'" **(Mark 10:29-31)**

I understood that God wants his servants to be blessed; not only on earth, but in the life to come too. We must not be men and women of God 'of association' that fill the transport vehicles and when the vehicles are ready to move, we remain. No, we have to be like Noah, enter also into the ark that God built by our hands. Do not win souls for the Kingdom of God and then lose our salvation because of some behavior. The Apostle Paul disciplined his body so that he would not be rejected after preaching to others!

Every person of God will give account to God for how they watched over the souls that were entrusted to them, "I have revealed you to those whom you gave me out of the world. They were yours; you gave them to me and they have obeyed your word. Now they know that everything you have given me comes from you. For I gave them the words you gave me and they accepted them..."

(John 17:6-8) And in this same way, the members also will give account to God concerning how they took care of the son of Levites; the priests of God.

Read a portion of the gospels where the judgment of the nations is spoken about by the son of man! **(Matthew 25:31-46)** While men of God serve you spiritually, you must serve them with natural things, even if they have activities that give them incomes.

When you get to Heaven, God will congratulate you for giving your leaders food, drinks, for covering them, for visiting them, taking care of them... because you have done this for one of the smallest of his children. This should not be a chore, but on the contrary, do it with joy. For all that you do, and I mean all the work you do for the advancement of the work of God on earth, it is written in heaven.

God will keep the records for those who are his children. What does John tells us in **Revelation 20:12?** "And I saw the dead, small and great, stand before God; and **the books were opened**. And *another book* was opened, which is the book of life: and the dead were judged out of those things which were written in the books, according to their works."

To go to heaven and to be saved, your name must be written in the book of life of the Lamb in the singular, "Anyone whose name was not found written in the book of life was thrown into the lake of fire." **(Revelation 20:15)**

Our name must be written in the book of life, but God also takes into account actions and all that we do for Him.

This is why the Bible speaks of books in the plural. Works follow us,

"... And the dead were judged according to their works, according to what is written in these books." Why does the Bible speak of books instead of a book?

This is simply because faith without works is dead. Abram, our father paid his tithe to Melchizedek, king of Salem, that is the tenth of all his income, **(Hebrews 7:1-2)** he offered his son Isaac on the altar. Rahab the prostitute was also justified through saving the lives of the spies sent by Joshua to Jericho and by making them to pass through another way to save their lives. You see that man is justified by works and not by faith alone! Our faith must be supported by our works. As the body without the soul is dead, so faith without works is dead. **(James 2:14, 20-26)**

God is asking you to support his servants so that they can fully play their role, "Will a man rob God? Yet ye have robbed me. But ye say, wherein have we robbed you? In tithes and offerings... Bring ye all the tithes into the storehouse, that there may be meat in mine house, and prove me now herewith, saith the LORD of hosts, if I will not open you the windows of heaven, and pour you out a blessing, that there shall not be room enough to receive it. And I will rebuke the devourer for your sakes, and he shall not destroy the fruits of your ground; neither shall your vine cast her fruit before the time in the field, saith the LORD of hosts. And all nations shall call you blessed: for ye shall be a delightsome land, saith the LORD of hosts." **(Malachi 3:8,10-12)**

Some will wonder whether men of God should work. Yes! This is true; serving God is not a mere game however, it is a work. One must be truly called of God to know the weight of this burden. God has always chosen his servants, and He has also paved the way for their source of income. After the deliverance of Israel, men of God, the instruments that God used, were not entitled to an inheritance. The Lord himself was their inheritance. But he asked that all the twelve tribes give a part of their inheritance to the Levites for their housing and suburbs for their cattle. They were to take care of everything what was spiritual and, in turn, the others would take care of them. **(Numbers 35:1-3 & Joshua 21: 41)** All the cities of the Levites within the possession of the children of Israel were forty and eight cities with their suburbs.

The children of Israel obeyed the Word of God. They accepted to take of their property and give it to the Levites.

Today in terms of spiritual warfare, Satan has hardened their hearts so it is very difficult for Christians to take a small portion of their property and give it to a man of God, a mission, a church, an NGO and so on.

What does **Proverbs 3:9-10** say? "Honor the LORD with your wealth, with the firstfruits of all your crops; 10 then your barns will be filled to overflowing, and your vats will brim over with new wine."

So then, honor the Lord with your substance. For who makes you different from anyone else? What do you have that you did not receive? And if you did receive it, why do you boast as though you did not? **(1 Corinthians 4:7)**

In summary, do not forget that God moved in your life by taking you out of your situation. He moved through someone who is close to you, his servant, so do not forget when God will visit you. This is what God explained to the children of Israel, on the eve of their departure from Egypt. He indeed asked them to kill a lamb and they were to roast it in the fire and eat it with unleavened bread and bitter herbs. **(Exodus 12:8)**

In the abundance symbolized by the flesh of the lamb and unleavened bread, God simply wanted to tell them not to forget the bitterness (difficult times) that they had experienced before he sent his servants to deliver them; that is the role of the bitter herbs.

If the people play their role, we believe that the men of God will be comfortable in the mission assigned to them in spiritual warfare. However, they also may have some lucrative businesses to support the work that God has entrusted to them as was the case of Paul, who was a tent maker!

What are the duties of the people of God vis-à-vis the warfare which sets at opposition heaven and hell? Indeed, it is for the people of God that I can call the Church to continue proclaiming the Word of God. God cannot be silent and it is through their mouth he wants to speak, "Surely the Sovereign LORD does nothing without revealing his plan to his servants the prophets." **(Amos 3:7)**

"I have also spoken by the prophets, and I have multiplied visions." *(**Hosea 12:11**) Before doing anything, God always takes the time to reveal it to his servants or to those who fear him, and will keep his covenant, "The LORD confides in those who fear him; he makes his covenant known to them." **(Psalm 25:14)** Is it not what happened with Abram when He wanted to destroy Sodom and Gomorrah?

"Then the LORD said, 'Shall I hide from Abraham what I am about to do?'" **(Genesis 18:17)**

Servants of the Lord, I think it's time for us not to work in scattered lines, we need one another!

Each at their post as Habakkuk describes. **(Chapter 1:1)** We will destroy the kingdom of darkness and the prayer of Jesus will be answered, "Your kingdom come, your will be done, on earth as it is in heaven." **(Matt. 6:10)** We can establish the kingdom of God on earth if each of us is conscious of the challenges of this spiritual warfare! It is our responsibility, our mission to proclaim the good news,

"He said to them, 'Go into all the world and preach the gospel to all creation.'" **(Mark 16:15)**

There are not two gospels, there is one. Whatever our call (apostle, prophet, teacher, evangelist or pastor **(Ephesians 4:11)**, we reveal God through our actions and our words. The Word is essential. If we preach it, God will confirm it through signs that will accompany it. It is an imperative precisely because it has not changed.

God needs you as a willing vessel. Even to the point of being like a donkey, offering a back He will ride on to be glorified.

Why should the Church preach the good news?

We will not talk of good news if things are normal, if they are as they should be. I think and I believe that it is because there is a problem that we have to give an announcement that will bring hope and joy to the heart of God's children. Each time men are attentive and they expect good news, there is already a bitter news. This is what happened in Samaria when it was besieged by Ben-Hadad, the king of Syria. The famine had reached such a peak that women, despite their tenderness and sensitivity, ended up eating their children. Isaiah was speaking to this when he said, "Can a mother forget the baby at her breast and have no compassion on the child she has borne? Though she may forget, I will not forget you!" **(Isaiah 49:15)**

At Samaria, women were made to forget the fruit of their womb, "As the king of Israel was passing by on the wall, a woman cried to him, 'Help me, my lord the king!' The king replied, 'If the LORD does not help you, where can I get help for you? From the threshing floor? From the winepress?' Then he asked her, 'What's the matter?' She answered, 'This woman said to me, 'Give up your son so we may eat him today, and tomorrow we'll eat my son.' So we cooked my son and ate him...'" **(2 Kings 6:26-29)**

I do not think there could be news worse than this. The king's ears were full and his heart was torn, this is why he tore his clothes in favor of a rag. **(verse 30)**

The king had to say something. He could not remain silent in such a battle. But he acknowledges his inability to solve such a problem! Someone could do it, one person; God! But this God had a representative; the Prophet Elisha. And the king was enraged that the Church was there, and could not change such poor news to a good word! "He said, 'May God deal with me, be it ever so severely, if the head of Elisha son of Shaphat remains on his shoulders today!' **(verse 31)** Before such a threat, Elisha, as the head representative of the Church felt compelled to release the words, "Elisha replied, 'Hear the word of the LORD. This is what the LORD says: About this time tomorrow, a seah of the finest flour will sell for a shekel and two seahs of barley for a shekel at the gate of Samaria.'" **(2 Kings 7:1)** The word was released and people were waiting for the good news; its fulfillment. But who did God choose to bring this good news? These are the lepers that were outside the city, because they did not allow them to stay within the city for fear of contamination. However, do not forget that scripture, "But God chose the foolish things of the world to shame the wise; God chose the weak things of the world to shame the strong. 28 God chose the lowly things of this world and the despised things—and the things that are not—to nullify the things that are," **(1 Corinthians 1:27-28)**

The Syrians heard the army of the Lord God coming against them and while fleeing, they could not take anything. It is the word of a prophet that is on God to fulfill. In spiritual warfare, people of God must release the word under the anointing of the Holy Spirit. Fulfillment, then, depends on God. "Who carries out the words of his servants and fulfills the predictions of his messengers, who says of Jerusalem, 'It shall be inhabited,' of the towns of Judah, 'They shall be rebuilt,' and of their ruins, 'I will restore them,'" **(Isaiah 44:26)**, "The LORD said to me, 'You have seen correctly, for I am watching to see that my word is fulfilled.'" **(Jeremiah 1:12)** When Elisha spoke this word, he went against those who besieged them and had its effect. All the work they have done, all their wealth and savings were for the Samaritans. "for the Lord had caused the Arameans to hear the sound of chariots and horses and a great army, so that they said to one another, 'Look, the king of Israel has hired the Hittite and Egyptian kings to attack us!' So they got up and fled in the dusk and abandoned their tents and their horses and donkeys. They left the camp as it was and ran for their lives." **(2 Kings 7:6-7)**

The outcast, the underrated, and the despised arrived in the city of Syria to eat, drink, and hide treasures and clothing. Those who, in principle, were destined to die cannot do anything with their fingers destroyed by leprosy, are the very ones whom God used to bring the good news to the city where they were despised and driven out, "Then they said to each other, 'What we're doing is not right. *This is a day of good news* and we are keeping it to ourselves. If we wait until daylight, punishment will overtake us. Let's go at once and report this to the royal palace.'" **(2 Kings7:9)**

Contrary to what was happening in Samaria, the lepers brought the good news! "And the people went out and plundered the Syrians camp." This is the good news that God wants us to announce, we his servants. What is this good news and what is its substance? This is what the angel of God said to the shepherds, "But the angel said to them, "Do not be afraid. I bring you good news that will cause great joy for all the people. Today in the town of

David a Savior has been born to you; he is the Messiah, the Lord." **(Luke 2:10-11)**

Here is the good news:

The birth of the Lord Jesus has come. This is what we must proclaim! Jesus is the new platform that God is evolving! Humanity must connect to Him or she will be outside the network and will not be able to capture the frequency of God! Satan has sufficiently traumatized the children of God throughout the world. "Proclaim the good news" of the birth of Jesus Christ. Let them know through the weapon of the word that there is someone who can save, deliver, heal... it is the person of Jesus.

Do You Know Why it Was Imperative for Jesus to Pass Through Death?

The answer is very simple; it is for the fulfillment of all the promises and will made for his beloved, his wife; which is the Church. See one or two promises,

"And I tell you that you are Peter, and on this rock I will build my church, and the gates of Hades will not overcome it. I will give you the keys of the kingdom of heaven; whatever you bind on earth will be bound in heaven, and whatever you loose on earth will be loosed in heaven." **(Matthew 16:18-19)**

"And these signs will accompany those who believe: In my name they will drive out demons; they will speak in new tongues; they will pick up snakes with their hands; and when they drink deadly poison, it will not hurt them at all; they will place their hands on sick people, and they will get well." **(Mark 16:17-18)**

The Church needs to be powerful and strong in order to resist the devil and cast out demons in the lives of God's children; transforming them by the word, impacting them, readjusting their mentality, and helping them to walk the plan and will of God. The only way for its achievement was death and God did not spare his Son. What did Paul tell us in **(Hebrews 9:16-17)?** "In the case of a will, it is necessary to prove the death of the one who made it, because a will is in force only when somebody has died; it never takes effect while the one who made it is living."

And Jesus Christ indeed died for you to be powerful in the propagation and the proclamation of His Word. He is waiting for you to seek for his children. As long as the Church has not touched all the nooks and crannies of the earth, the Son of Man cannot rapture His elect.

God is counting on you! He has not changed His strategy concerning his servants. Since creation he works through men to bring a change in the lives of His childrens' distress. In Egypt, to deliver Israel from the suffering the Egyptians subjected them to, He came down, "The LORD said, 'I have indeed seen the misery of my people in Egypt. I have heard them crying out because of their slave drivers, and I am concerned about their suffering. 8 So I have come down to rescue them from the hand of the Egyptians and to bring them up out of that land into a good and spacious land, a land flowing with milk and honey...'" **(Exodus 3:7-8)**

To achieve this purpose that was burning in his heart for Israel, God came down certainly, but in spirit. He incarnated Moses by his spirit so that he could serve as a channel, "And now the cry of the Israelites has reached me, and I have seen the way the Egyptians are oppressing them. So now, go. I am sending you to Pharaoh to bring my people the Israelites out of Egypt." **(Exodus 3:9-10)**

Moses could not go before Pharaoh, that great terrible and powerful king of his time! And God will give him a guarantee, "I will be with you…" **(Exodus 3:12)** but Moses, a man like us was afraid to confront this terrible king. He ignored the power of God in the battle he had to deliver against Egypt and their kings. He seeks for another excuse, "O my Lord, I am not eloquent…but I am slow of speech, and of a slow tongue." However, despite this resistance, the choice of God to deliver Israel from Egypt was Moses, because it was not in vain that God allowed him to grow up in the Egyptian territory with the Egyptians kings.

God used the experiences that Moses had to make him a better instrument that could deliver His children. So, to solve the resistance of Moses, God would send his brother Aaron, who was also a Levite, servant of God. But in all this conversation that Moses had with God, there are some elements that we note and that we should not neglect. It is the Word of God in the mouth of his servants,

"The LORD said to him, 'Who gave human beings their mouths? Who makes them deaf or mute? Who gives them sight or makes them blind? Is it not I, the LORD? Now go; I will help you speak and will teach you what to say.'" **(Exodus 4:11-12)** "You shall speak to him and put words in his mouth; I will help both of you speak and will teach you what to do. 16 He will speak to the people for you, and it will be as if he were your mouth and as if you were God to him." **(Exodus 4:15-16)**

God will speak through our mouth to bring His children out of their situation. In Egypt, it was Moses and Aaron that he used; in Babylon, He listened to the prayers of Daniel to liberate Israel from the Babylonian captivity **(Daniel 1:6, 9:2-3)** was Samson not chosen to begin the deliverance of Israel from the hands of the Philistines? **(Judges 13:1-5)** to kill Goliath and give victory to Israel, did God not take David, despite his young age? **(1 Samuel 17:16-19 and 50-53)** did the Midianites not met God on their way by the channel of Gideon? **(Judges 6:6, 8, 28)** was Elijah not sent to the widow of Sarepta? **(1 Kings 17: 8-16)** was Elisha not been a blessing to the woman of Shunem? **(2 Kings 4:1-17)** did God not anoint Jephthah to liberate his people from the hand of the son of Ammon? **(Judges 11:29-33)** was Peter not sent to preach to Cornelius, a Gentile and his family? Although there have been outpourings of the Holy Spirit in Acts 10, to confine ourselves to these examples.

When we look back, we need to understand that the Old Testament is a shadow of the reality that will be fulfilled in the New Testament. The Old Testament is a partial fulfillment of the New Testament! God's blessing can be available to men that believe at the cross of CHRIST! Before the death of Christ, men could be heirs of the blessing only under the law, which were their guardian and governor. But the fullness of the inheritance after the death of Christ is governed by the Spirit. This is how Jesus Christ trained his disciples before passing through death, then resurrection, because it was impossible that death should hold him in hell; he will promise the Holy Spirit. When the disciples received him, the first thing they did was to proclaim the Word of God! Thus men like apostles Peter and John, Philip, James etc., will continue to proclaim the Word of the Lord that is to say, the Good News. Today, Peter is not around to go to Cornelius' house in Caesarea to proclaim the Good News, neither is John, not to talk of the great Apostle Paul. But you and I are here. God is counting on us to represent Him correctly. We must preach the message of the Cross not only as the center of history, but also and especially the starting point of salvation of the human race that is the basis of our teaching!

If we receive the grace of God, without doing anything, so we receive it in vain. The Bible says, "Seek the LORD while he may be found; call on him while he is near." **(Isaiah 55:6)** It is now that we have the opportunity to be committed in the ministry of the Word of God: Christ died for all humanity! This is the foundation! Each of us should know how he will build on this foundation. There is no other foundation! Did Paul not warned us in 1 and 2 Timothy, because the spirit of the two books is the same, flee from legalism, the gossip, fables and doctrines of demons and continue firmly in the direction of faith and love,

"The goal of this command is love, which comes from a pure heart and a good conscience and a sincere faith." **(1 Timothy 1:5)**

In short, the Word of God must not cease to be proclaimed, it is a very important weapon, if we are silent, the souls will not know the truth and consequently, cannot be freed,

"Then you will know the truth, and the truth will set you free." **(John 8:32)**

For men to be saved, they must call upon the name of Lord. "for, 'Everyone who calls on the name of the Lord will be saved.' How, then, can they call on the one they have not believed in? And how can they believe in the one of whom they have not heard? And how can they hear without someone preaching to them?" **(Romans 10:13-14)**

May God help us to preach His Word and demonstrate His power by the Holy Spirit. **SMITH WIGGLESWORTH** prophesied on **three movements of God during this century:**

First, that of the Spirit with the demonstration of the power of God

Secondly, that of the Word with teachings that edifies and finally

Thirdly, the combination of the first two that of the Spirit and the Word.

With this last point, we can make much progress and exploits. As much as God speaks through us, as much as He confirms His Word by the signs that accompany it. If he did it with the first disciples, we know that He has not changed, he will do the same with us! It is for us to rise up and play our own role: preaching the Good News and Him, He will play His role: to demonstrate His power, **"Then the disciples went out and preached everywhere,**

and the Lord worked with them and confirmed his word by the signs that accompanied it." (Mark 16:20)

Miracles agree, but first the Word! If the Word is preached in all the truth, God will demonstrate His power through manifestations of His Spirit. We should not ignore that all miracles do not necessarily come from God! When God sent Moses with miracles, God demonstrated His power, but the magicians and enchanters of Pharaoh also did miracles. Their rods were also transformed into snakes but not by the power of God! However, the GOD of the Word 'I am that I am' was eventually shown victorious by His servant Moses whose snake swallowed the other snakes. It is the Word that will give us discernment to know the name of the god that so-and-so operates their miracles through.

Do not forget that we are in a battle against an ingenious evil opponent! Miracles are not weapons of spiritual warfare although they are very important for strengthening of our faith. Our fathers have seen miracles, signs, and all kinds of works wrought by God in the wilderness, but they did not know the ways of God. **(Psalm 95:8-10)** As for the Word of God, it is a very powerful weapon that should in no way be diverted! It is the word that apart from information brings transformation!

The Source of the Word

Men are who they are. They seek always to develop the letter to the detriment of the spirit. They will create all kinds of philosophies, doctrines, and literatures in order to make the Word of God powerless. But we people of God have one thing; we are ministers of a new covenant. Not of letter, but of the Spirit; for the letter kills, but the Spirit gives life. **(2 Corinthians 3:6)**

It is the Spirit of God, who will now give us the Word of God so that we can communicate it to the people of God. Do not give spiritual scraps to the wonderful people for which Jesus Christ came to give His life on the cross. No, otherwise God himself will lead them to another place with vibrant, green pastures!

Henceforth, where do we find this word? Not on earth, but in heaven! Men with their evil thoughts are capable of anything so God has set His Word in heaven, "Your word, LORD, is eternal; it stands firm in the heavens." **(Psalm 119:89)** One should be in the presence of God to receive His Word. Anyone who wants to go beyond the 'Logos' which is the written word, must enter into the reign of God to receive the 'Rhema' the revealed word. Jesus said to Peter, "Blessed are you, Simon son of Jonah, for this was not revealed to you by flesh and blood, but by my Father in heaven." **(Matthew 16:17)**

The Almighty God who made the heavens his throne revealed himself to those faithful to him and gave them instructions, "The LORD confides in those who fear him; he makes his covenant known to them." **(Psalm 25:14)**

Brothers, we must go up to the mountain of revelation where besides 'Logos,' God communicates to us the 'Rhema' as he did with Moses when he spent time in his presence on the mountain! Indeed, Moses did not only receive the two tables of the Ten Commandments, but he again exchanged with God. To insure this, he went to the top of the mountain. This was where the true revelation that gives life to the written word rested; for it becomes a living word capable of, "...dividing soul and spirit, joints and marrow; it judges the thoughts and attitudes of the heart." **(Hebrews 4:12)**

Listening to such words or preaching, it seems our ears have never heard anything like it. Reading the words from the page, it seems that our eyes have never seen. And they never entered our heart! **(1 Corinthians 2:9)** Is this not why the Apostle Paul could say, "My message and my preaching were not with wise and persuasive words, but with a demonstration of the Spirit's power, 5 so that your faith might not rest on human wisdom, but on God's power." **(1 Corinthians 2:4-5)** To achieve this, it is essential to be in his presence.

This is very simple to understand:

If the Word of God is settled in heaven, you must go up there to get it. Listen to these words, "I know a man in Christ who fourteen years ago was caught up to the third heaven. Whether it was in the body or out of the body I do not know—God knows. And I know that this man— whether in the body or apart from the body I do not know, but God knows— was caught up to paradise and heard inexpressible things, things that no one is permitted to tell." **(2 Corinthians 12:2-4)**

It is not permissible for anyone to hear these ineffable words, only those who know how to wait for God to hear his voice can benefit. The Word of God is a mystery, and only those who are called by God and do His Will can receive the revelation of this mystery, "He replied, 'Because the knowledge of the secrets of the kingdom of heaven has been given to you, but not to them.'" **(Matthew 13:11)** These are Jesus' words to his disciples. The Apostle Paul did not say the opposite,

"...that is, the mystery made known to me by revelation, as I have already written briefly." **(Ephesians 3:3)**

Yes, there are leaders in the faith, people of God, and real teachers who have received the mysteries; you just have to learn from them, receive teachings, and the true Word of God to preach the true Christ.

The people need this mystery; to support people of God by praying that they receive the revelation,

And pray in the Spirit on all occasions with all kinds of prayers and requests. "With this in mind, be alert and always keep on praying for all the Lord's people. Pray also for me, that whenever I speak, words may be given me so that I will fearlessly make known the mystery of the gospel," **(Ephesians 6:18-19)**

The mystery of the Gospel is the Good News that we find in **John 3:16, "For God so loved the world that He gave His only begotten Son that whosoever believeth in Him should not perish, but he has eternal life."**

Jesus Christ is the mystery that we must reveal, "I want you to know how hard I am contending for you and for those at Laodicea, and for all who have not met me personally. My goal is that they may be encouraged in heart and united in love, so that they may have the full riches of complete understanding, in order that they may know the mystery of God, namely, Christ, in whom are hidden all the treasures of wisdom and knowledge." **(Colossians 2:1-3)** We are then, anointed to preach Christ **(Isaiah 61:1-3)** because it is in Him that we find all the grace of God, the fullness, the anointing, life, power, authority, being, and all the treasures of God **(Ephesians 4:7)** We should preach him alone.

The Authority of the Word of God

We have already said a little earlier that the Word of God is God Himself. This means we should respect the authority of the Word, which He reveals to his servants. A man of God filled with the Word of God- I mean 'Logos,' the written word and the 'Rhema,' the revealed Word- is no longer an ordinary man! He has God in him. He is pregnant with the Word of God as Mary was pregnant with the son of God, the living word. While he is not God meaning not be worshipped as God is, he contains or exists as a little god. Do not forget that our God is a consuming fire; therefore His servant can be for us a blessing if we really want to follow the words that God has put in his mouth. At the same time, it can be a danger to us if we challenge the authority that God has granted.

A man truly called of God, when he preaches, teaches, or prophesies, is led by God's Spirit, who communicates His words, "When Jeremiah had finished telling the people all the words of the LORD their God — **everything the LORD had sent him to tell them." (Jeremiah 43:1)**

It was not the words of the prophet Jeremiah, but the Word of the Lord God in the mouth of his prophet, it was fire. Jeremiah the prophet did not want at a time in his life to speak on behalf of God because of his suffering and persecutions. But he could not help but speak on His behalf!

Why?

Because nobody can contain God in himself, He is the Word and He must come out! Every man of God must give birth as Mary did. The Word of God should not and cannot know an abortion, "Whenever I speak, I cry out proclaiming violence and destruction. So the word of the LORD has brought me insult and reproach all day long. 9 But if I say, "I will not mention his word or speak anymore in his name," his word is in my heart like a fire, a fire shut up in my bones. **I am weary of holding it in; indeed, I cannot." (Jeremiah 20:8-9)**

When a man of God speaks to a nation, a people, a family, or even an individual in the name of the Lord, (I am not talking about just any words, but when he speaks in the name of the Lord) we must forget our diplomacy, our title, our position, and our certificates electing to submit instead to the authority of the Word of God! The word that comes from the mouth of the true servants of God has the same power and the same authority as if it came directly from the mouth of God! It is not in vain that God said concerning David that he is the man after His heart. It is not that David never sinned, he simply recognized the authority of the Word of God from the mouth of the servants of the LORD.

When he took Bathsheba, the wife of Uriah, the Hittite, to be his wife, and he killed his rival by the sword of the son of Ammon, God revealed himself to him by the canal of his servant Nathan and David recognized his sin. By acknowledging it he recognized the authority of the Word of God in the mouth of Nathan; this is why he repented.

Men of God are carriers of God messages. The thought, the word, and the will of the heartbeat of God to his people, "For prophecy never had its origin in the human will, but prophets, though human, spoke from God as they were carried along by the Holy Spirit." **(2 Peter 1:21)**

God can make any of his servants a god for nations, peoples, families, or individuals that he sends them to. This was the case of Moses, "Then the LORD said to Moses, 'See, I have made you like God to Pharaoh, and your brother Aaron will be your prophet.'" **(Exodus 7:1)** This is simply because God had put his authority in the mouth of Moses and Pharaoh in spite of its obstinacy, was obliged to submit to the will of God the Creator. The battle was between Moses, the servant of God, and Pharaoh, worker of the devil, because he did not serve God. Despite his resistance, Israel after four hundred and thirty years was able to find the way to freedom! **(Exodus 12:42)**

Hallelujah!

Also in his ministry, at some point, men rose up against the authority of Moses (or rather against the authority that God had delegated to his servant Moses.) It was a mistake not to commit because Satan used three protagonists in this battle against the man of God, namely Korah, Dathan and Abiram died the way Moses asked the Lord, "'But if the LORD brings about something totally new, **and the earth opens its mouth and swallows them**, with everything that belongs to them, and they go down alive into the realm of the dead, then you will know that these men have treated the LORD with contempt.' As soon as he finished saying all this, the ground under them split apart and the earth opened its mouth and swallowed them and their households, and all those associated with Korah, together with their possessions." **(Numbers 16:30-32)**

The authority is in the mouths of men of God, it is for us to take advantage. When the prophet Eli spoke in a hard way to Hannah, she was careful to reply the prophet because she knew in his mouth, God had put authority she needed for her miracle, "Hannah was praying in her heart, and her lips were moving but her voice was not heard. Eli thought she was drunk and said to her, 'How long are you going to stay drunk? Put away your wine.'

'Not so, my lord, Hannah replied, 'I am a woman who is deeply troubled. I have not been drinking wine or beer; I was pouring out my soul to the LORD. Do not take your servant for a wicked woman; I have been praying here out of my great anguish and grief.'" **(1 Samuel 1:13-16)**

Faced with such self-control and humility, Eli could only release authority, "Eli answered, 'Go in peace, and may the God of Israel grant you what you have asked of him.'" **(Verse 17)** That same year, she became pregnant and she bore a son, whom she named Samuel.

When we read also the Gospel of Matthew, we find an exciting story, that of a Canaanite woman who cried to Jesus in relation to her daughter who was tormented by demons. First, Jesus answered her with not a word. Then, Jesus said, "I have been sent to the lost sheep of the house of Israel." Thirdly, Jesus affirmed finally, "It is not meet to take the children's bread and cast it to dogs." The woman knew what she wanted. She was aware of the authority that was in the mouth of Jesus.

She wanted to get a word from him that would bring healing to her daughter and not attract a curse. What mattered to her was the authority of the Word that Jesus would release and because of her tenacity, she was able to get it.

Listen a little to her word, after all the reactions of the Lord,

"Truth, Lord, yet the dogs eat of the crumbs which fall from their masters' table." Jesus was 'forced' to release the word that would bring the miracle, "O woman, great is your faith! Be it unto you even as you wilt."

It is not everyone who hears such a word!

Only those who recognize the authority of the Word of God -this creative word- that calls into existence what does not exist. This word is the word by which all things were created. Jesus spoke and the same hour, her daughter was healed **(Matthew 15:21-28)**

When we speak of the authority of the Word of God, we speak also and at the same time of the authority of the men of God. Indeed, they are filled with the Word of God, which is God and is full of authority. They also automatically receive this authority as it becomes a part of their persons.

Peter, by his word and in the name of the authority that God had given him, healed Aeneas, a paralytic lying on his bed for eight years. And this same Peter resurrected

Dorcas named Tabitha. See how Peter used his authority in both cases:

"As Peter traveled about the country, he went to visit the Lord's people who lived in Lydda. There he found a man named Aeneas, who was paralyzed and had been bedridden for eight years. 'Aeneas,' Peter said to him, 'Jesus Christ heals you. Get up and roll up your mat.' Immediately Aeneas got up. All those who lived in Lydda and Sharon saw him and turned to the Lord. In Joppa there was a disciple named Tabitha (in Greek her name is Dorcas); she was always doing good and helping the poor. About that time she became sick and died, and her body was washed and placed in an upstairs room. Lydda was near Joppa; so when the disciples heard that Peter was in Lydda, they sent two men to him and urged him, 'Please come at once!' Peter went with them, and when he arrived he was taken upstairs to the room. All the widows stood around him, crying and showing him the robes and other clothing that Dorcas had made while she was still with them. Peter sent them all out of the room; then he got down on his knees and prayed. Turning toward the dead woman, he said, 'Tabitha, get up.' She opened her eyes, and seeing Peter she sat up." **(Acts 9:32-40)**

Elijah also released the authority, and for three and a half years, rain did not fall. **(James 5:17)**

As for Paul, he used his authority several times to make known the Lord Jesus Christ to his contemporaries. This was the case with the magician Elymas named Bar-Jesus, who opposed the conversion of deputy Sergius Paulus. Paul asserted his authority and the magician was stricken with blindness. That was enough for the proconsul to accept the Lord Jesus. **(Acts 13:4-12)** In all these things, we must have discernment and know the time of our visitation.

The Time of Visitation

The time of visitation is also another way of knowing the time when God comes through the channel of his servants to change the course of our history. A man of God who goes to a family, goes in principle to accomplish a mission. It is up to the family to know that it is God, who is visiting through his servant. It took a long time before Israel realized that it is God who had sent Moses to deliver them from the hand of Pharaoh! Certainly, the task was not easy for Moses and the collaboration was not easy, but in return, they too suffered until God was gracious to them. It is for this reason, you need to know when God comes to visit you so that you may open your heart and the man of God may accomplish his mission; to teach you the Word of God that will touch your spirit, and give meaning to your life.

We think incorrectly- and this is a trick of the devil in spiritual warfare- that because the man of God is not financially comfortable, he cannot be a source of blessing to us.

Watch out, God chose the lowly things to confound those things that are considered and the weak things to confound the mighty! **(1 Corinthians 1:27)** Do not look at the external adornment, weigh instead the spiritual level with eyes of discernment. Naaman was the leader of the Syrian army. He probably had the largest military uniforms, but under his uniform there was leprosy that gnawed. It is said that clothes do not make the man! There are true servants of God who really want to be a blessing to the people of God. They can certainly be needy, but if the spirit convinces us, receive them and allow them to do the work for which God has sent them. However, be very careful because all those who present themselves as the servants of God, are not necessarily servants of God! There are present wolves in sheep's clothing.

Have discernment. Through their word, they are discerned and through their fruit, they are recognized.

Many people have no discernment and reject outright the men of God. They may be right with all the bad testimonies we have here and there concerning men of God!

However, wanting to close his eyes to avoid seeing a malefactor, our benefactors can pass us unnoticed. Elijah had a twofold need:

One, he was thirsty and

Two, he was hungry.

At the house of the widow of Zarephath, despite his anointing, his authority and power that God gave him, he was subjected to demand. There are things he needed but this did not prevent the wife from receiving him. Imagine for a moment if she had refused to receive Elijah, her miracle would not be possible and she would have lost or missed her time of visitation. But glory be to God, she received Elijah as needed, and in turn, he played the role for which God had sent him. **(1 Kings 17:8-24)** If Elijah were not present, the son of this woman would have died.

But she first received him before receiving the visible or apparent proof that he was a true servant of God.

"Then the woman said to Elijah, 'Now I know that you are a man of God and that the word of the LORD from your mouth is the truth.'" **(Verse 24)**

In the same vein, Elisha was sent to a woman who had no child. In fact, God wanted to visit the woman, she therefore, needed the Word of God from the mouth of a servant of God. Do not forget that we are talking about the Word of God in spiritual warfare as a weapon. In fact, the Shunamite woman received Elisha and his spiritual son Gehazi, firstly, Elisha ate in the house of the same woman whenever he passed by;

secondly, the Shunammite woman consulted her husband after discernment and together they gave an upper chamber for his retirement, a bed, a table, a chair and a candlestick. She knew the time of her visitation for accepting God's anointed into her house during his time of retirement. The consequence is that Elisha released the word in relation to the couple's need and the miracle took place; she had a son. **(2 Kings 4:8-37)**

Let us make a point, spiritual warfare requires people of God. In the last two illustrations, death came knocking for the two children that was that of the widow of Sarepta and that of the Shunammite both, by the channels of the men of God which are Elijah and Elisha, father and spiritual son, the children came back to life. If God blessed us and we stay in touch with those he used for us, Satan could not snatch our blessing. The same servants will raise their voice and God will listen. Because when God blesses, there is no sorrow, "The blessing of the LORD brings wealth, without painful toil for it." **(Proverbs 10:22)**

When you do not know the time of your visitation, longer stays than expected in Egypt occur. That is not the will of God. In principle God intended that the children of Israel to stay for 400 years but they spent 430 years in Egypt. They consoled themselves (in suffering that was too long) as the brothers said it was, "our time of wilderness."

Yes there is a time that we pass through the wilderness, but it is not throughout eternity, we must one day come to the promised land, where milk and honey flows. After 400 years, the people of Israel made no effort to come out of the situation. We must recognize the time of our visitation, because as God passes on land, he sees the suffering of human beings, and he wants to intervene to ease us. Let us then open our eyes and lift up our arms so that he can help us through his servants. Jesus, when approaching the city of Jerusalem could not hold back his tears! Why? He saw the misery which hit the city for lack of knowing the time of their visitation, "As he approached Jerusalem and saw the city, he wept over it and said, 'If you, even you, had only known on this day what would bring you peace—but now it is hidden from your eyes. The days will come upon you when your enemies will build an embankment against you and encircle you and hem you in on every side. They will dash you to the ground, you and the children within your walls. They will not leave one stone on another, because you did not recognize the time of God's coming to you.'" **(Luke 19:41-44)**

May God help us to know our time in obedience to His word.

In summary, the Word of God cannot at all be in the background. It is unavoidable in spiritual warfare. Apostles, Prophets, Evangelists, Pastors, and Teachers, we have to teach because God gave us His Church for the perfecting of the saints! **(Ephesians 4:11-13)** It is the same with our words, we cannot neglect them. It must be positively affected by the Word of God because it also plays a role in the realm of the spirit.

<u>Our Own Words</u>

Do you know that there is a power in your mouth? Your tongue!

It's able to do many things in the realm of the spirit especially in our daily battle. The greatest blessing or curse a man can pronounce on himself or on others emanates from his mouth, "Out of the same mouth come praise and cursing. My brothers and sisters, this should not be." **(James 3:10)** This means that the tongue plays a strategic role in spiritual warfare. I understand why the word was the first work that God gave to man. We have already spoken about it.

Brethren, let me tell you that the devil uses our own tongues to destroy us. It's surprising to hear children of God say certain things to themselves or to their offspring or partners:

"I'm dead."

"I cannot succeed."

"My life is over."

"This child is the devil."

"My children are headed nowhere fast."

"My spouse will never change."

"You are Satan!" The list goes on and on…

Ignorance is a disease. Now that we are trying to heal it by the light of the Word which produces knowledge, you must never say that. Do not say such things, neither on yourself nor on your children or your partner. It is a trick of the devil to destroy you. What does Proverbs say? **"The tongue has the power of life and death, and those who love it will eat its fruit." (Proverbs 18:21)** It is not the tongue itself that causes the problem, "Even fools are thought wise if they keep silent, and discerning if they hold their tongues." **(Proverbs 17:28)** It is the product that comes from the tongue, the result is good word. And the Bible says, **"Death and life are in the power of the tongue."** This perfectly describes what the tongue can do.

How many parents have destroyed the lives of their children by cursing them through the power of the tongue?

During colonization, many families spoke words on their children (incantations) for them not to do well in school so that white men will not take them, but for them to return to the village and stay with them. And if all these words are not broken by other words this time positive word, not only will they continue to act, but they will always continue.

Why? Just because the words are seeds that once thrown into our spirit, grow roots, sprout, grow and bear fruit. Jesus once said in John, "The Spirit gives life; the flesh counts for nothing. The words I have spoken to you—they are full of the Spirit and life." **(John 6:63)** Do not play with words, they are spirit and life.

You can start right now to use your weapons to break any word that was pronounced against you and is acting against your life, your home, your work etc.

If someone curses you in your presence, refuse and reject all these curses! If it is a person you can respond to aloud for the person to know that you have rejected these bad seeds, do this and prophesy good words into your life while the person is there. It can sound simple, but it is very important. If it is a person you do not have the right to speak freely around, be silent and lead the battle in your spirit in silence without even opening your mouth or moving your lips.

In your spirit, you refuse and you reject it and once you are in a better place to speak, break all the evil the person prophesied and prophesy positively on your life.

It must be done.

Very often the children of God who do not ignore it, and know the effect of the word, break the evil words pronounced on their lives. But their knowledge was not complete; they would not speak on, after breaking, what they want from God. Whenever you break a negative word, your tongue has the power of pronouncing another positive word into your life. When farmers cut down trees and clean up the space, they put the seed they want in the ground. It may be corn, wheat, millet, or soya. Regardless of what it is, they throw something in the ground **(Jeremiah 1:10)**

You can live of course in reality but this reality should not prevent you from saying what you want to happen to you in your life. The word that you say is important. One day, it will eventually become a reality and will change the present reality that you did not want. This is why I often say that reality is not always the truth. You live in a difficult situation which is the reality, but not the truth because the truth is what God said about you that will come to pass. Confess and declare it until the fulfillment.

In **1 Samuel, chapter 17,** David realized these things despite his young age. There was indeed a war between Israel and the Philistines, and the people of God lived in a harsh and frightening reality for forty days.

The reality is that the Philistine hero named Goliath kept them in fear through the words of his mouth. Every day, morning and evening, he uttered the same words and there was no one, no one to answer him nor battle against him. Thus when David arrived at the battlefield, being sent by his father Jesse in order to give food to his three brothers who followed Saul to the war he was able to witness the reality as it was. The defiant words of Goliath would fall into the ear of David. He quickly inquired about the benefits, the privileges, and the rewards that he would receive if he was the man to take the life of this strong, tall, and terrifying man.

After getting answers to his questions, he decided to fight Goliath. But before the battle took place physically, it was first spiritual. It is what happened in the spiritual that is reproduced in the natural! Goliath tries to kill David with his mouth professing the name of his gods, his fetishes, and talisman like many people do in the spiritual to hurt their opponents,

"He said to David, 'Am I a dog, that you come at me with sticks?' And the Philistine cursed David by his gods. 'Come here,' he said, 'and I'll give your flesh to the birds and the wild animals!'" **(Verses 43-44)**

But David refused this seed of death and all curses of Goliath. He initially opposed the two gods outright, that his God is the true, "David said to the Philistine, 'You come against me with sword and spear and javelin, but I come against you in the name of the LORD Almighty, the God of the armies of Israel, whom you have defied.'" **(Verse 45)** Then David relied on his God, the LORD of hosts, to declare his victory over Goliath, **"This day will the LORD deliver you into mine hands,"**

I can imagine David saying with confidence and certainty,

"This day the LORD will deliver you into my hands, and **I'll strike you down and cut off your head.** This very day I will give the carcasses of the Philistine army to the birds and the wild animals, and the whole world will know that there is a God in Israel. All those gathered here will know that it is not by sword or spear that the LORD saves; for the battle is the LORD's, and he will give all of you into our hands." **(verse 46-47)**

For the first time, and after forty days' domination, Goliath met someone who answered him. This put him in a state of anger, and without responding to David, he set himself in motion against him. It was sure he would lose the battle because it was David who had the words of victory when the battle started.

Goliath was dead well before his death; the words of David killed him spiritually before the stone or the sword killed him physically. This is what the witches do. They kill first in the spiritual before the death occurs in the natural world. This is why one ought always to pray using the armor of God.

Moreover, David acted as he had said; he killed Goliath with a stone and a sling, cut off his head with the sword that he pulled from the sleeve of his fallen opponent, because he himself did not have any other weapon.

With the victory of David over the hero Goliath, the men of Judah and Israel pursued the Philistines and overcame them. When a hero rises, he raises those behind him, several other heroes.

May the Lord make us heroes who will kill the Goliaths that stand against our nation, our people, our country, or our family.

Amen!

Brethren, in spiritual warfare, we must speak. The Bible even said that there is time for all things under heaven, a time to be silent, but also a time to speak. **(Ecclesiastes 3:1, 7)** If it is time to speak, you do not have the right to remain silent.

History teaches us that Africa was colonized, but a time came when black men like Houphouet BOIGNY, Leopold SENGHOR, Kouame N'KRUMAH, and Sekou TOURE spoke with the colonizers, discussed freedom with them until the time came for independence. If we also want to enter our spiritual, financial, physical, and marital independence, it is time to open the mouth and make declaration. We must talk, it is a must! Do you have a business opportunity? Do you want something unique for your station in life? Are you suffering from any sickness of which you want to be healed from? Talk to those around you so that they can help you.

When Haman made a death edict against the Jews living in the kingdom of Ahasuerus, the Jews heard this, they had the Fast of Esther which went three days and nights without food or drink.

The book of Esther told us clearly, "And in every province, whithersoever the king's commandment and his decree came, there was great mourning among the Jews..." and what did they do? "They were fasting, and weeping, and wailing; and many lay in sackcloth and ashes." **(Esther 4:3)** All this is to invoke God. But he still had to talk to someone that God was willing to use to unblock the situation and solve the problem. It turned out to be the king. And the person who could do it through her strategic position was Esther. In a situation after fasting and praying, we must talk to people that God will use to help us. Elisha told the widow to request for empty vessels from her neighbors. These are our relationships, they are important in this spiritual warfare, and we must not neglect them. Because Esther did not understand these things, Mordecai opened her spiritual ears to convince her to talk to King Ahasuerus!

I can imagine Mordecai telling Esther, "We have all finished fasting and praying, God will do what we ask him, but you also as a woman have your part to play. Speak to the king and God will act through him." He can go on according to verses 13 and 14, "Do not think that because you are in the king's house you alone of all the Jews will escape. For if you remain silent at this time, relief and deliverance for the Jews will arise from another place, but you and your father's family will perish. *And who knows but that you have come to your royal position for such a time as this?*" **(Esther 4:13-14)** These words will push Esther to take her responsibilities to save Jews from death. God answered their prayers, because the king stretched out his golden scepter to the queen, synonymous with grace. The king himself will ask repeatedly what she wanted, even to the half of his kingdom; he became a lamb.

In short, God turned the king's heart in favor of the Jews after the queen spoke with him.

Do you want a job? Do you have a trip planned? Are your business endeavors blocked?

Speak!

Esther spoke, "If I have found favor with you, Your Majesty, and if it pleases you, grant me my life—this is my petition. And spare my people—this is my request. For I and my people have been sold to be destroyed, killed and annihilated. If we had merely been sold as male and female slaves, I would have kept quiet, because no such distress would justify disturbing the king." **(Esther 7:3-4)**

The rest of the story tells us that Haman, the enemy of the Jews, was hanged upon the gallows he had prepared for Mordecai. But despite this death, Esther continued to speak for their lives were not completely spared. Haman's edict sealed with the ring of the King should be revoked so that Jews can feel good and be comfortable and live their lives, "Esther again pleaded with the king, falling at his feet and weeping. She begged him to put an end to the evil plan of Haman the Agagite, which he had devised against the Jews." **(Esther 8:3)** If you can speak and table the problem, there will always be a solution. Even if she was rewarded by the king for her bravery, do not forget that the king himself gave the house of Haman to her. Esther did not think of herself alone, she thought about her race located in the provinces that may have been destroyed by the effects of letters written by Haman but sealed by the king's ring. She was successful, not only that the letters of Haman were revoked, but the king added, "Now write another decree in the king's name in behalf of the Jews as seems best to you, and seal it with the king's signet ring—for no document written in the king's name and sealed with his ring can be revoked." **(Esther 8:5 and Esther 8:8)**

This is how the Jews were saved in all the 127 provinces, located in India to Ethiopia.

In spiritual warfare, if you do not speak, you are delaying yourself or blocking your own progress. There are situations before which the word is mandatory. Even if the situation is as hard as a stone, if you have a pain in the heart, if you are in the valley of the shadow of death, yes, even if all you see seems to prove the contrary, speak positive, declare the word of faith. Certainly, Abraham was called the father of faith, but he first spoke to the servants before going on the mountain,

"He said to his servants, 'Stay here with the donkey while I and the boy go over there. We will worship and then we will come back to you.'" **(Genesis 22:5)** His word was a weapon and knew how to use it.

Mary was called the mother of Jesus, but when the angel Gabriel finished talking to her, despite the fact that it was incredible and impossible she said, "I am the Lord's servant," Mary answered. 'May your word to me be fulfilled.' Then the angel left her." **(Luke 1:38)** The angel waited to leave Mary after holding a word from her. Your angel that God has sent is still close to you. Hum something, tell him what you want before he goes to give account to the One who sent him.

"Then the man said, 'Let me go, for it is daybreak.' But Jacob replied, 'I will not let you go unless you bless me.'" **(Genesis 32:26)** Jacob said what he wanted. He was sure to say what was on his heart while the angel of the Lord was with him. The result is obvious; the angel of God blessed him. Your responding word is important in the battle you engage in to succeed in your life.

However, we are not saying to children of God to speak anywhere and anyhow. There are moments where you must speak to settle your situation and at the same time, there are moments when you have to remain silent so that you will not open up your secret to your enemy or your opponent.

In this moment, you can opt for the weapon of a silent word which is thought.

<u>Our Thinking</u>

Again, there is a problem because people ignore that they are the fruit of their imagination. And instead of thinking positively and seeing yourself great, people feel sorry for themselves and allow themselves to become imprisoned by their thoughts. You must know that your thoughts and your imaginations are also a weapon in spiritual warfare! You are not the fruit of accident, but you were brought forth with intention and purpose. Yes, God the creator first thought of you in his mind before he created you, "Then God said, "Let us make mankind in our image, in our likeness, so that they may rule." **(Genesis 1:26)** It suggests that God first created man in His mind; in His 'Head' and imagination before he became real in the natural world.

And it is true, your purpose is to dominate! Brother dominates your mind. God created you from His mind; it is your turn to recreate from your own thought.

The Apostle Paul draws our attention to this fact, "Whatsoever things are true, whatsoever things are honest, whatsoever things are just, whatsoever things are pure, whatsoever things are lovely, whatsoever things are of good report; if there be any virtue, and if there be any praise, think on these things." **(Philippians 4:8)**

All our thoughts must be submitted and held captive to the obedience of Christ **(2 Corinthians 10:5)** Leave no part to the enemy. As soon we have unhealthy, negative, and defeatist thoughts, we open the way for demons. This is why any thought that is not according to the Word of God that goes through our mind must be rejected automatically. In the word 'imagination' we have the word 'Image'. When you make a projection into the future from your mind, what image do you have of yourself? If you see yourself as great, prosperous, and powerful, you can continue the battle until total victory. The opposite is not obvious!

As long as your thought is negative, you will not have the strength to continue the battle. I think that everything we use was first in the minds of the people who invented them. The bed, the chair, the table were first in thought- in the spirit of the carpenter- before existence was realized in the physical world. All these beautiful houses that we have existed first in spirit before being built into nature.

The Building engineers can tell you without a doubt how the house will be after construction and at the end, what you will see will be the exact copy of their plan. Why? Because before building, they have the plan, shapes, and sizes all in their head well before they are put it on a frame. In spiritual warfare, Satan is aware of these spiritual realities so he attacks the man from his mind in hopes that he will not achieve his objectives. In your mind, how do you see yourself? In your thought, who are you? Do you constantly sense these flaws in relation to your thought? Is your mind in a spiritual prison? I want to inform you that a spiritual prison is the most dangerous of all prisons that may exist. If your spirit is trapped in the prison of your thought, until it is released, your success is impossible. You must be passionate about your destiny before it can happen.

Your spirit must be truly free and your thought positive. It means that even if your body is in jail, while your thoughts are positive, you will end up coming out of the prison because your spirit is free.

This is what happened with Paul and Silas. Although their bodies were imprisoned, their spirits were free. They walked outside and had no fear. Is that not why, unlike the other prisoners, they sang praises to God and prayed during the night? **(Acts 16:25)**

Be free in your spirit. See yourself great and you will secure the victory. Joseph was sold by his brothers, but this man was attached to the dreams, nocturnal visions, and interpretations that God revealed to him. He knew in his spirit that God was not a man to lie, nor the son of a man to repent of His word. Joseph protected his thoughts to ensure he always kept positive. One day, he would find himself as the head of his family revealed as their 'savior!'

Joseph spent time in Potiphar's house, an officer of Pharaoh and captain of the Egyptian guard. Joseph thought his dreams would now come to fulfillment. To the unbeliever his dreams appeared an illusion because he ended up in jail at the hands of Potiphar's wife. There could be very few situations that were worse to imagine. But notice it is merely a physical prison. He never allowed his spirit to be imprisoned by a negative thought. The proof is that inside the prison, he explained the dreams of others and waited faithfully for his own to come true. This is the reason he told the chief butler of the king who was in the same cell with him, "But when all goes well with you, remember me and show me kindness; mention me to Pharaoh and get me out of this prison." **(Genesis 40:14)**

Joseph knew in his spirit that he could not die in prison and he knew also that Pharaoh would one day need him, "…and make mention of me unto Pharaoh, and bring me out of this house." The rest of the story tells us literally that Pharaoh needed Joseph to explain his dreams and his butler was the instrument that God used to establish this connection. Joseph had already experienced these things in his imagination and I'm sure he was not surprised when it happened in his life.

Are you free in your mind? Be free! Let the truth free your mind and it will set you free! **(John 8:32)**

2 Corinthians tells us, "Now the Lord is the Spirit, and where the Spirit of the Lord is, there is freedom." God wants you to be free in your spirit. Accept Him and you will see his Spirit gives spiritual energy to your spirit to keep your thoughts positive and your imaginations great. This is what happened with Abram. He was living a reality; he had no child. God would act on the negative thought he built in his spirit. So God fortified some walls that held his lesser thoughts captive. What did God do? "He took him outside and said, 'Look up at the sky and count the stars—if indeed you can count them.' Then he said to him, 'So shall your offspring be.'" **(Genesis 15:5)** This is where God increased and strengthened the faith of our father Abraham. He changed his thought and imagination. This image is engraved in his mind. He could

say every day, shuddering, 'My seed shall be as the stars of heaven.' God won and that is what he also wants to do with us.

But before we continue, let me tell you that it is not in vain that advertising spaces are expensive. Advertising is fixed on one objective; to awaken the minds of consumers in relation to a particular product!

Take one or two examples:

If anyone is thirsty, he thinks on how to take a refreshment such as mineral water or a soft drink and so on. Moreover, once the clothes are dirty, to do the laundry, we think immediately of a soap according to the image that our mind registered in the moments of advertisements. Whatever you may be going through, have a good thought! Engrave good images on the table of your mind as they will reinforce your thoughts when times are dire.

Consider again the word that God said to Abram,

"'Look up at the sky and count the stars—if indeed you can count them.' Then he said to him, 'So shall your offspring be.'"

Do you not see that the word 'such' marks an analogy, a comparison? Let's develop a pattern of going back to the Word of the Lord, "'Count the stars, if you can count them. The way they are numerous, this is the same way your children will be numerous.' Abram believed the LORD, and he credited it to him as righteousness." **(Genesis 15:6)**

Have confidence also in the Lord to maintain your positive thought. If you are in the prison of your mind,

Christ will set you free. This is one of the reasons he came down from heaven,

"The Spirit of the Sovereign LORD is on me, because the LORD has anointed me to proclaim good news to the poor. He has sent me to bind up the brokenhearted, to proclaim freedom for the captives and *release from darkness for the prisoners.*" **(Isaiah 61:1, Luke 4:19)**

Here, I think it is spiritual prison rather than physical prison. Jesus Christ wants to free our minds so that the enemy will not use it against us in spiritual warfare, "For Christ also suffered once for sins, the righteous for the unrighteous, to bring you to God. He was put to death in the body but made alive in the Spirit. After being made alive, he went and made proclamation to the imprisoned spirits…" **(1 Peter 3:18-19)**

If you hear the voice of Christ through these lines, even if your spirit is imprisoned or dead, you will experience Resurrection, "Very truly I tell you, a time is coming and has now come when the dead will hear the voice of the Son of God and those who hear will live." **(John 5:25)** It is not in vain that the scripture says, "This is why it is said: 'Wake up, sleeper, rise from the dead, and Christ will shine on you.'" **(Ephesians 5:14)**

Your resurrection from the dead speaking spiritually was made possible by the death of Jesus, "And when Jesus had cried out again in a loud voice, he gave up his spirit." **(Matthew 27:50)** "… and the tombs broke open. The bodies of many holy people who had died were raised to life." **(Matthew 27:52)**

We prophesy the resurrection of your spirit and the deliverance of your mind. Refuse the notion that your mind will be used as a base where the enemy lands to destroy you. The children of Israel had this problem and God was obliged to deal harshly with them so their mentality would be renewed and changed. This is true for the Jews as the family of Jacob that went to Egypt were seventy people in number **(Genesis 46:27)** but when they came out of Egypt, they were no longer a family; they had become a nation as God had predicted, "'I am God, the God of your father,' he said. 'Do not be afraid to go down to Egypt, for I will make you into a great nation there.'" **(Genesis 46:3)**

Still, in their minds, the Jews had a mentality of family. They saw themselves small and powerless. Their suffering and affliction in Egypt make them to lose all hope. Despite their large numbers, they see as a family unable to do anything. In his strategy, God would allow them to meet the people of Amalek. Do not forget that Amalek was a nation and was also the first nation to speak as Balaam. **(Numbers 24:20)** War would begin between Israel and Amalek, and Israel would win through in the hands of Moses that was lifted and strengthened by Aaron and Hur. God used Amalek as a nation to change the minds of the children of Israel. **(Exodus 17:8-13)** Through the hands of Moses, God conveyed a message, "As long as Moses held up his hands, the Israelites were winning, but whenever he lowered his hands, the Amalekites were winning." **(Exodus 17:11)**

He said to Israel, you are a nation, raise your spirits and fight. If your thought remains captive in the battle, and your hands refuse to fight, Amalek is a nation and it will defeat you. Israel understood the lesson, and fought. And the result was a defeated Amalek.

Henceforth, Jews now know that they are a nation. God also wants you to fight in your mind, from your mind, and by your mind so that you will get the victory.

The people of God should know that they can succeed and will succeed but should not be locked up in the net of poor thought. Whenever God wants to act, He starts by transforming our way of thinking. When the people of Israel were greatly impoverished because of the Midianites and God wanted to deliver them, he sent his angel. But the angel worked first on the spirit of Gideon; the instrument that God would use,

"The Lord is with you, mighty man of valor. Go in this your might, and deliver Israel from the hand of Midian have I not sent you?" This was not easy for the angel, he had fulfilled his mission to change the way of thinking and the vision of Gideon. Listen to Gideon, "And he said unto him, 'Oh my Lord, wherewith shall I save Israel? behold, my family is poor in Manasseh, and I am the least in my father's house.'

And the LORD said unto him, 'Surely I will be with you, and you will smite the Midianites as one man.'"

Gideon would still ask to make an offering. And this time, the angel after accepting the offering would disappear so as to mark the spirit of Gideon by this strong image. The same night Gideon would begin his work in his own homeland; destroying all the idols according to the order of the Lord! After that, the history tells us that Gideon won the victory over the Midianites.

God is ready to do the same thing with us. He wants to destroy all the walls of Jericho that are hindering us from our blessings. But it is up to us to open the door of our heart, "Here I am! I stand at the door and knock. If anyone hears my voice and opens the door, I will come in and eat with that person, and they with me." **(Revelation 3:20)**

God is a God of principle. If we walk according to his principles, we will have the same results as our fathers who have preceded us in faith. If he listened to Abram, Gideon, Paul, and Silas, he will listen to us and bring us into our destiny. Even if things go wrong and God says, 'All is well,' keep your mind stayed on what God has said. It implies that the miracle has happened in the spiritual world. It is a matter of time. Walk with the eyes of the spirit. By faith, I mean, and not by sight. God is not interested in the darkness, what he thinks is what he said, "And God said, 'Let there be light,' and there was light." **(Genesis 1:3)**

Do you think it is in vain that Moses, despite his place in Egypt, agreed to leave their territory to join the people of God in the wilderness? He knew in his spirit and in his mind that the future reserved for him with Israel would be more glorious than he had in the house of king Pharaoh. It was a question of mentality.

If your mentality changes, your thought is transformed and your attitude will also change automatically. The image affects the way we think and our behavior. You are the image of what you see, of what you look forward to, and what your spirit keeps in your mind. You have an interest in keeping good thoughts. Make a good choice, "This day I call the heavens and the earth as witnesses against you that I have set before you life and death, blessings and curses. Now choose life, so that you and your children may live." **(Deuteronomy 30:19)** God wants you to live happy, and with prosperity; not only you, but you and all your posterity. However, be also ready as Satan always attacks those who are free in their mind. You have to resist him and you will have the victory. Amen!

Nowadays, we have people who can inspire us by the way they maintain their positive thinking. Their mind attaches to future realities despite the present they live within.

NELSON MANDELA spent many years in prison! Although a prisoner, I am sure and certain that he saw in his mind leading the great South Africa! Time has proved him right.

ABDOULAYE WADE spent how many years in search of the Senegalese presidential seat! In his mind, he saw himself sitting on the chair by the ballot box and not by hijacking his way. History has proved him right. It is not only perseverance but the state of mind.

One does not pass through dangerous shortcuts when our mind has lost the battle and even the war.

OBASANJO of Nigeria spent a time in prison and he suffered atrocities. There are marks of his affliction even on his body! But he knew one day he would take over the reins of the presidency. Time has proven him right.

Do not throw in the towel; fight in your mind to refuse any defeatist idea and continue the battle. One day, and again I say one day, you will also give testimony and people will appreciate God from your experience. Still, we cannot be great in society without having a solid foundation. You need a cluster of experience to better manage what God wants to give you.

Keep your head up to the heaven, the throne of God, for he will provide everything you need on earth, "Abraham lifted up his eyes," "I will lift up my eyes…" **(Genesis 22:13, Psalm 121:1)**

For all those who lifted up their eyes, their thoughts to the Lord eventually gave testimonies. It's your turn to say all what God has done for you, if you can keep your thoughts positive.

May God help us to understand all these realities of spiritual warfare and protect us from neglecting the effectiveness of the weapons he has given us.

The mistake that many children of God make is to ignore the effectiveness of the weapons that God has put at their disposal. That's why they seek other powers that are only satanic powers, which can only help them for a short time. Do not forget that the devil is the father of lies! **(John 8:44)** If you refuse to use weapons given by God, you will be obliged in spiritual warfare to seek for a small ring, a small charm, a small amount of magic powder, a small chain, demonic books, or the like. None of these can equal or even come close to the weapons that God, in His love, has given you.

Pray with the name of Jesus and the Blood of Jesus, quote the Word of God, and invoke the Holy Spirit to the changing of your word and your mind. Know that these weapons are not to be neglected. **"For though we live in the world, we do not wage war as the world does. 4 The weapons we fight with are not the weapons of the world. On the contrary, they have divine power to demolish strongholds." (2 Corinthians 10:3-4)**

These weapons are mighty through God to the pulling down of strongholds.

By the power of God:

The Name of Jesus chases demons

The blood of Jesus neutralizes the powers of darkness

The Word of God disarm the enemies

The Holy Spirit pulls down the strongholds of disease, infertility, curses, spiritual slumber, of unemployment, chronic poverty and so on...

Our own word and our thoughts make us become what we are supposed to be. It is by the virtue of God that we can successfully fight the devil and confirm the victory that we have on him through the death and resurrection of Jesus Christ.

Before closing this chapter, it is important to emphasize a fact. We are all engaged in spiritual warfare without exception, whether we want it or not. Satan came down on earth! Spiritually speaking, we are all on a journey. To be successful, we must use the weapons that God has given us, "Therefore put on the full armor of God, so that when the day of evil comes, you may be able to stand your ground, and after you have done everything, to stand.

Stand firm then, with the belt of truth buckled around your waist, with the breastplate of righteousness in place, and with your feet fitted with the readiness that comes from the gospel of peace. In addition to all this, take up the shield of faith, with which you can extinguish all the flaming arrows of the evil one. Take the helmet of salvation and the sword of the Spirit, which is the word of God." **(Ephesians 6:13-17)** Be aware, while we are engaged in full battle, our protection is ensured by our God; the excellent Protector!

Daniel Buraimo

Chapter 4
The Protection
In Spiritual Warfare

God never said that the war would not take place. His word is clear on it, "They will fight against you," declares the LORD but what is certain is that, "but [they] will not overcome you," why? "'for I am with you and will rescue you,' declares the LORD." **(Jeremiah 1:19)**

"When you pass through the waters, I will be with you; and when you pass through the rivers, they will not sweep over you. When you walk through the fire, you will not be burned; the flames will not set you ablaze. For I am the LORD your God, the Holy One of Israel, your Savior; I give Egypt for your ransom, Cush and Seba in your stead." **(Isaiah 43:2-3)**

Since society is governed by laws, the powers of evil act spiritually to do you evil that they cannot do physically.

This makes spiritual warfare inevitable. Know that everyone is not able to prepare for or celebrate your success. You must remain silent at times to secure your promise and avoid oversharing, even among your varied friend circles.

You cannot tell a sorcerer not to attack you, it is his job! He must attempt and he must fail so that he can know your God is the most excellent protector!

Yes, there will be terrors of the night, arrows that fly by day, the pestilence that walketh in darkness, and the destruction that wasteth at noonday. **(Psalm 91:5-6)** Yes, there will be weapons forged against you to break your home, your financial life, or your health. Yes, there will be tongues that will rise up against you, but if you take refuge in the LORD, you will know as well as your enemies and adversaries that the name of the Lord Is truly a strong tower! **Proverbs 18:10** says, "The name of the LORD is a fortified tower; the righteous run to it and are safe."

You have a legacy of protection from the Lord, **"no weapon forged against you will prevail, and you will refute every tongue that accuses you. This is the heritage of the servants of the LORD, and this is their vindication from me," declares the LORD." (Isaiah 54:17)**

You do not have to be afraid of all these evil powers. They are working for their master; the devil called Satan. But be not afraid as the latter is no bigger than your God who created you. You know that the devil is the father of lies; in reality, he knows he can do nothing against you but he makes you afraid to snatch your victory or at least to make you doubt your inheritance! "...for he [the devil] is a liar and the father of lies." **(John 8:44)** Slightly close your eyes, imagine God close to you, and listen to His word addressed to you, "So do not fear, for I am with you; do not be dismayed, for I am your God. I will strengthen you and help you; I will uphold you with my righteous right hand. 11 "All who rage against you will surely be ashamed and disgraced; those who oppose you will be as nothing and perish. 12 Though you search for your enemies, you will not find them. Those who wage war against you will be as nothing at all. 13 For I am the LORD your God who takes hold of your right hand and says to you, Do not fear; I will help you. 14 Do not be afraid, you worm Jacob, little Israel, do not fear, for I myself will help you," declares the LORD, your Redeemer, the Holy One of Israel." **(Isaiah 41:10-14)**

You know that God cares for you and your protection concerns Him. Why are you fearful or afraid when He is near you? Take to heart the adage that said, "Whoever is on the back of the elephant is not afraid of the dew."

Listen! The fearful die before their death! Do not accept that fear kills you before the time that God has given you. The Bible says, "Submit yourselves, then, to God. Resist the devil, and he will flee from you." **(James 4:7)** Even if you feel a danger or an attack, remain calm and unruffled, have faith in Him and He will intervene. David knew this well, "The LORD is my shepherd, I lack nothing." **(Psalm 23:1)** "Yea, though I walk through the valley of the shadow of death, I will fear no evil: for you art with me; your rod and your staff they comfort me." **(Psalm 23:4)**

With God, the LORD of hosts, you will not lack protection. Whenever you feel the need, call upon Him. He is the most excellent protector! He neither slumbers nor sleeps. Because of His faithfulness in the battle, Jeremiah cried in front of his enemies, "**But the LORD is with me as a mighty terrible one!**" And if God is with him, what is the consequence, "But the LORD is with me like a mighty warrior; so my persecutors will stumble and not prevail. They will fail and be thoroughly disgraced; their dishonor will never be forgotten." **(Jeremiah 20:11)** Amen!

Let's look at how God protects His children that we are.

The Blood of The Lamb

We have already seen the Blood of Jesus as a weapon in spiritual warfare, but it is also an undeniable protection. God gave Jesus so that His blood can play a protective role before the myriad people who besiege us on all sides! When a child of God accepts Jesus, he is automatically covered by the Blood of Jesus. As he enters into the covenant represented by the sacrifice of Jesus on the Cross, the demons cannot touch or hurt him. This is why you should call upon your God every day. He will cover you and all your possessions with the Blood of Jesus and, by His grace, you will see the resulting peace.

When God sent Moses to Egypt, Pharaoh resisted nine plagues. The tenth was the death of the firstborn. So that Israel would not be affected by this plague, God asked them to do something, "Tell the whole community of

Israel that on the tenth day of this month each man is to take a lamb for his family, one for each household." **(Exodus 12:3)** "Then they are to take some of the blood and put it on the sides and tops of the doorframes of the houses where they eat the lambs." **(Exodus 12:7)**

Some will ask why get the doors dirty with the blood? It is the epitome of spiritual response and has a much deeper meaning. The Bible said, "The person without the Spirit does not accept the things that come from the Spirit of God but considers them foolishness, and cannot understand them because they are discerned only through the Spirit." **(1 Corinthians 2:14)**

I pray that you will not receive this as man derived from the animals or consider this mystery in the natural, but as a spiritual being so that you can understand spiritual things. Blood in effect, was to serve as a sign, "The blood will be a sign for you on the houses where you are, and when I see the blood, I will pass over you. No destructive plague will touch you when I strike Egypt..." **(Exodus 12:13)** "When the LORD goes through the land to strike down the Egyptians, he will see the blood on the top and sides of the doorframe and will pass over that doorway, and he will not permit the destroyer to enter your houses and strike you down." **(Exodus 2:23)**

The blood was a mark distinguishing the Hebrews and the Egyptians. The children of Israel, unlike their enemies, were to be spared, "At midnight the LORD struck down all the firstborn in Egypt, from the firstborn of Pharaoh, who sat on the throne, to the firstborn of the prisoner, who was in the dungeon, and the firstborn of all the livestock as well. Pharaoh and all his officials and all the Egyptians got up during the night, and there was loud wailing in Egypt, for there was not a house without someone dead." **(Exodus 2:29-30)**

Spread the blood of Jesus over your house, your car and on everything you have. You declare in the natural and it happens in the spiritual world.

But why the Blood of Jesus?

The answer is simple.

To deliver Israel from Egyptian captivity, God used the blood of a lamb to ensure their protection. The Blood of the Lamb that was slain is the image of the Blood of Jesus that was shed for us! It is for this that John the Baptist did not hesitate to say, "Behold the Lamb of God." Jesus is the Lamb of God and you need spiritually speaking to be marked by the blood on your forehead, "Do not harm the land or the sea or the trees until we put a seal on the foreheads of the servants of our God." **(Revelation 7:3)**

I urge you to refuse to cooperate with the devil opting to instead accept the protection through the blood that was shed for you. Once you have Jesus, your spiritual body is marked by the blood of the Lamb and your days and nights are protected! There is another, protective role of Holy Spirit in the battle we are engage in spiritually.

The Holy Spirit

The Holy Spirit protects the children of God in various ways. We need to be sensitive to how He works and the uses of the Holy Spirit for protection.

Fire

The Holy Spirit is symbolized by fire and protects us in 1001 ways. God as a devouring fire makes us flames of fire. If someone wants to touch us, the fire that we are will burn him and we are secured, "He makes winds his messengers, flames of fire his servants." **(Psalm 104:4)**

Elijah understood this mystery of protection through fire. Indeed when the king of Israel was ill, he sent messengers to consult the god of Ekron named Baal-Zebub to know if he will cure him of his disease. Elijah the Tishbite sent back Ahaziah, the king's messengers, with bitter news, "But the angel of the LORD said to Elijah the Tishbite, "Go up and meet the messengers of the king of Samaria and ask them, 'Is it because there is no God in Israel that you are going off to consult Baal-Zebub, the god of Ekron?' Therefore this is what the LORD says: 'You will not leave the bed you are lying on. You will certainly die!'" So Elijah went." **(2 Kings 1:3-4)**

After receiving the Word of the Lord by the mouth of the messengers, king Ahaziah sent a captain of fifty along with his fifty men to seek for Elijah and bring him! What was the intention or the thought of the king? Only God knows. One thing is certain however; the two groups that were sent one after the other were subjected to the same fate, "Elijah answered the captain, 'If I am a man of God, may fire come down from heaven and consume you and your fifty men!' Then fire fell from heaven and consumed the captain and his men. At this the king sent to Elijah another captain with his fifty men. The captain said to him, 'Man of God, this is what the king says, 'Come down at once!" 'If I am a man of God,' Elijah replied, 'may fire come down from heaven and consume you and your fifty men!' Then the fire of God fell from heaven and consumed him and his fifty men." **(Verses 10-12)**

Fire came down from heaven and verse twelve states the Fire of God came down from heaven as the day of Pentecost in Acts 2:3, "cloven tongues like as of fire..."

Elijah consumed his enemies. If God answered by fire, it was to preserve the life of his anointed who had not yet finished his mission on earth. If you invoke the God who answers by fire, in the same way He listened to Elijah, He will listen to you. His fire will consume your enemies so that you can be in peace. Your life is precious in the sight of the living God. You can cry to Him, "Lord, Lord God who is a consuming fire, I pray you Father to send down now, this very hour your fire on my enemies! Let your fire consume all of them without exception! That all their projects of destruction, their arsenals, their bases, their hiding places, their meeting places, and any other things they use against me and my family are consumed by your fire in the name of Jesus."

Do not be more spiritual than God, who agrees to answer by fire. Say this prayer with me again, "Lord, let your anger kindled against those who are fighting against me, and your fire kindle among them and devours all their camp by the power of your spirit in the name of Jesus," **(Numbers 11:13)** "Lord, that the enemies that gather underwater for meetings against me, my life, my work, my marriage, my home, and my children be scattered. As your word dictates, **you boil the bottom of the water** where they gather in the name of Jesus." **(Job 41:22)** Amen!

If you have to be alive to fulfill your prophetic destiny, you need to be protected! This occurs through the wind of the Holy Spirit which acts to ensure our safety.

The Wind

"He [God] makes the winds His messengers." **(Psalm 104:4)**

"Suddenly there came a sound from heaven as of a rushing mighty wind." **(Acts 2:2)**

Let us remember one thing:

When we talk about the protection of God, it's all that God does, by all the means that he uses so we can be protected and

safe so as to achieve the goal of our existence. When God acts through the wind, it is for specific missions. Please, empower yourself to call upon God and He will blow different winds relating to our need, "He makes the winds His messengers." Before obstacles, impossible cases, we can cry to God to blow the east wind. This wind comes from the desert, (Syro-Arabian) "Even though he thrives among his brothers. An east wind from the LORD will come, blowing in from the desert; his spring will fail and his well dry up. His storehouse will be plundered of all its treasures." **(Hosea 13:15)** It is recognized by its length and its duration, "So Moses stretched out his staff over Egypt, and the LORD made an east wind blow across the land all that day and all that night. By morning the wind had brought the locusts;" **(Exodus 10:13)**

It blows to hurt the opponent. The east wind carried locusts into Egypt. **(Exodus 10:13-15)** When God occupies your enemy, the enemy becomes entangled and no longer has time for you; he must expend energy to come out of his misfortune.

This is the wind that the LORD blew on the Red Sea to split it; allowing the people of God to pass through before engulfing their enemies, "Then Moses stretched out his hand over the sea, and all that night the LORD drove the sea back with a strong east wind and turned it into dry land. The waters were divided," **(Exodus 14:21)**

This is the same wind that blew on Jonah when he wanted the destruction of God's people located in Nineveh, "When the sun rose, God provided a scorching east wind, and the sun blazed on Jonah's head so that he grew faint. He wanted to die, and said, 'It would be better for me to die than to live.'" **(Jonah 4:8)** When you are against the people of God, whoever you are, God can in His wrath bring the east wind to give you a serious correction or even death.

Heed this politicians, and all men whether or not you be servants of God: Do not make the people to whom God sent His Son Jesus to suffer, otherwise He can still make the wind to blow to protect his children that he loves so much.

Also in this impulse of love, God will stand in favor of His children. If we call upon him, he will blow west wind from the west to sweep everything ravaging the land and our blessings. Do you know that there are spiritual moths as well as pests to devour your blessings? God wants to act through the west wind and displace them, but before that, He awaits your obedience,

"And we will be ready to punish every act of disobedience, once your obedience is complete." **(2 Corinthians 10:6)**

When your obedience is complete, his wind will blow to remove all destruction and protect your assets. In Egypt, when God made the east wind to blow to harm Egyptian, this east wind brought grasshoppers, "So Moses stretched out his staff over Egypt, and the LORD made an east wind blow across the land all that day and all that night. By morning the wind had brought the locusts;" **(Exodus 10:13)** These locusts had a mission, "They covered all the ground until it was black. They devoured all that was left after the hail—everything growing in the fields and the fruit on the trees. Nothing green remained on tree or plant in all the land of Egypt." **(Exodus 10:15)** Having seen the damage that the locusts caused, Pharaoh 'repented.'

"Pharaoh quickly summoned Moses and Aaron and said, 'I have sinned against the LORD your God and against you. Now forgive my sin once more and pray to the LORD your God to take this deadly plague away from me.'" **(Exodus 10:16-17)** When Pharaoh was yielded to the will of God, God answered the prayer of His servant Moses, making a wind blow; specifically the west wind, "And the LORD changed the wind to a very strong west wind, which caught up the locusts and carried them into the Red Sea. Not a locust was left anywhere in Egypt." **(Exodus 10:19)**

The west wind is very strong, but fast. No grasshopper, no fever, and no moth can stand against this wind. I pray that God will do it to liberate your blessings that the enemy has devastated. Our God is a God of order. After casting out the devourer, we must have tangible things and blessings to continue on living our life. In that moment, the wind He elects to send is called 'the south wind.'

While the children of Israel were walking in the desert, God provided water from the rock to quench their thirst and rained manna wheat from heaven to feed them. However, they still murmured against God and His servants when they wanted to eat meat. Instead of murmuring, they could have prayed or simply informed Moses. Their attitude displeased God. And you know what he wanted to do? He wanted to bring the east wind to hurt them, "He did blow in the heavens the east wind."

Notice one thing: When the east wind blows, it comes with correction; an affliction against a person, a group of people, or a population. But in His love and mercy, God repented of his anger and by His power, quickly sent another wind to meet the needs of the people, "He let loose the east wind from the heavens and by his power made the south wind blow." **(Psalm 78:26)**

In heaven, He makes the wind blow from the East, but he did not send it. The wind He brought by His power is the south wind. The south wind is a wind that gives birth; birthing material blessings as well as spiritual, "He let loose the east wind from the heavens and by his power made the south wind blow. *27* He rained meat down on them like dust, birds like sand on the seashore. *28* He made them come down inside their camp, all around their tents. *29* They ate till they were gorged— he had given them what they craved." **(Psalm 78:26-29)**

I pray that the Lord make his wind to blow from the south to provide answers to the needs of the people of God, in the Name of Jesus!

Amen!

One thing to remember is that our Heavenly Father will do everything for our protection, and that we may perform; the reason for our creation. It is incumbent on us then to trust Him and remain attached to Him. When there was flood, Noah stayed for a long time on the face of the waters. He did not, however, doubt for a moment God's faithfulness, "The waters flooded the earth for a hundred and fifty days." **(Genesis 7:24)**

But in due course, the God of heaven responded in Noah's favor, "But God remembered Noah and all the wild animals and the livestock that were with him in the ark, and he sent a wind over the earth, and the waters receded." **(Genesis 8:1)**

There are waters that hindered the stability of our ark, our life, our work, our home, and our finances. This is just as the ark of Noah was unstable on the face of the waters. In such a situation, God sends a wind. The Bible was not precise, it simply said, "God made a wind to pass over the earth."

It is warfare and so it may take the time that it will take, but one thing is certain, the water will dry up by the wind, "The water receded steadily from the earth. At the end of the hundred and fifty days the water had gone down," **(Genesis 8:3)**

I call this wind the 'wind of God's memory.' He sends it as soon as his children are in danger according to His memory, "God remembered Noah, and God sent a wind."

I prophesy that God will remember you, and make blow the wind so that your ark can settle and that your life will be in security, to the glory of His name. Amen!

Do not forget that we are engaged in spiritual warfare. This is a war in which the enemy also kicks, scratches, and fights! He did not declare himself defeated, He also continues on fighting fight and you know, he is a good imitator! We already know the role of the devil on earth, "The thief comes only to steal and kill and destroy…" **(John 10:10)**

He also blows a wind in his way against the children and servants of God. Was it not his wind that blew against the wall to kill Job's children, "While he was still speaking, yet another messenger came and said, 'Your sons and daughters were feasting and drinking wine at the oldest brother's house, when suddenly a mighty wind swept in from the desert and struck the four corners of the house. It collapsed on them and they are dead, and I am the only one who has escaped to tell you!'" **(Job 1:18-19)** The wind that took the life of the children of Job were not of God but the devil. The east wind is a wind from the LORD, and the Bible says it comes from the desert and not the other side of the desert **(Hosea 13: 15)** Behold how Satan imitates and blows destructive winds in families. That is why we must have discernment to threaten and stop the demonic spirits that act behind these winds.

The example of Jesus is instructive. In fact, when he crossed the sea with His disciples, there was a great storm with waves that beat into the boat so that it was filled with water. The disciples were frightened and asked for His help. How did He react? "He got up, rebuked the wind and said to the waves, 'Quiet! Be still!' Then the wind died down and it was completely calm." **(Mark 4:39)**

When Jesus said to the wind, 'Peace, be still,' he was taking authority over evil spirits. It was proved in Mark, where Jesus had same reaction in the face of a man who had an unclean spirit, "'Be quiet!' said Jesus sternly. 'Come out of him!'" **(Mark 1:25)**

You can take authority over every wind sent by the devil blowing in the opposite direction of your boat. You can also continue to pray asking the Lord to blow the four winds of heaven against your opponents to divide them. **(Daniel 11:4)**

But for you, He should make His Spirit to blow from the four winds so that your dry bones can come back to life, and your spiritual, financial, material, health, and marital 'deaths' can experience a resurrection so that the glory can go back to God Almighty! Amen! **(Ezekiel 37:9)**

Moreover, the Spirit of God by his anointing ensures our protection. If the Holy Spirit inhabits us as children of God, the Spirit produces heat that neutralizes the missiles of the enemy. 1 John told us, "You, dear children, are from God and have overcome them, because the one who is in you is greater than the one who is in the world." **(1 John 4:4)** The question to know and understand is "*Who* is in you?" Some will say it is Jesus. This response is not false but it lacks complexity and therefore is incomplete. It is Jesus who lives in us by his Spirit. Jesus has ascended into heaven, "After he [Jesus] said this, he was taken up before their very eyes, and a cloud hid him from their sight." **(Acts 1:9)**

The Spirit who dwells in us is God Himself and, as you know, no power, no spirit, no agent of the devil, nor the devil himself could compare either near or far to Him. Do you know why the three Hebrew boys— Shadrach, Meshach and Abednego— did not die in the fiery furnace of the Babylonian king, Nebuchadnezzar? God, by His Spirit with them, neutralized the heat of the fire by another heat greater than that of the fiery furnace! The smell of fire did not reach the companions of Daniel, nor the fire itself, "And the satraps, prefects, governors and royal advisers crowded around them. They saw that the fire had not harmed their bodies, nor was a hair of their heads singed; their robes were not scorched, and there was no smell of fire on them." **(Daniel 3:27)**

Unlike the Hebrew, the Babylonian children who accepted to bow down before the statue of gold did not benefit from the heat of the Holy Spirit. Consequently, they were killed by the flames or the heat of the fire.

God knows how to protect us. He may bring trials and even difficulty, but He always ensures our protection if we belong to Him! If Jesus said, "I am sending you out like sheep among wolves. Therefore be as shrewd as snakes and as innocent as doves." **(Matthew 10:16)** This does not mean that He abandons us. Quite the contrary, "And surely I am with you always, to the very end of the age." **(Matthew 28:20)**

Christ is spiritually present through his Spirit to protect us. This is the message He gave to the disciples in a coded form, "On one occasion, while he was eating with them, he gave them this command: 'Do not leave Jerusalem, but wait for the gift my Father promised, which you have heard me speak about.'" **(Acts 1:4)** It is after this, after you have received the Spirit, "But you will receive power when the Holy Spirit comes on you; and you will be my witnesses in Jerusalem, and in all Judea and Samaria, and to the ends of the earth." **(Acts 1:8)**

Explain a Mystery:

The Mystery of The Anointing And The Spirit

All the children of God are anointed with something specific that they are required to do on earth. John the Baptist revealed this to his disciples, "A person can receive only what is given them from heaven." **(John 3:27)** If you succeed on the earth in a field or in many things, it is because you got it from the heaven. It is a mark which was put on you by the Creator and it is your anointing! Some can say, 'but you learn before you know!' This is true, but remember that it is not everyone that masters all that he or she learn! And besides, who are the first men who taught them how to do all these wonderful works? It is God in them, through His anointing placed on them on their spirit. Let read Exodus together, "Then Moses said to the Israelites, 'See, the LORD has chosen Bezalel son of Uri, the son of Hur, of the tribe of Judah, **and he has filled him with the Spirit of God, with wisdom, with understanding, with knowledge and with all kinds of skills— to make artistic designs for work in gold, silver and bronze, to cut and set stones, to work in wood and to engage in all kinds of artistic crafts. And he has given both him and Oholiab son of Ahisamak, of the tribe of Dan, the ability to teach others. He has filled them with skill to do all kinds of work as engravers, designers, embroiderers in blue, purple and scarlet yarn and fine linen, and weavers—all of them skilled workers and designers.'"** (Exodus 35:30-35)

You see that it is God who gives these gifts and it is He who brands His children and allows that they can teach the gifts to others who have predispositions. Even with an earth full of people, so does he brand each by a specific anointing. He said to Jeremiah, "I sanctified you, and ordained you a prophet unto the nations," When? "Before I formed you in the belly." **(Jeremiah 1:5)**

But this anointing on us is revealed with the power of the Holy Spirit for those who want to follow God. People will offer methods of passing through by other means. This I cannot advise for those who want to go to heaven after life on earth.

Regardless, when we pray, fast, and listen to the Word of God, the anointing melts like butter in the sun and it reveals what we are. In fact, the Spirit of God descends and heats the brand that is on us, and we are able to achieve what is necessary to exteriorize what is hidden in us! Speaking in a simplified way, the Spirit comes after anointing and it is the Spirit through the fire that reveals the anointing. What did Jesus say in Luke, "The Spirit of the Lord is on me, because he has anointed me to proclaim good news to the poor. He has sent me to proclaim freedom for the prisoners and recovery of sight for the blind, to set the oppressed free" **(Luke 4:18)**

I pray that God reveals the anointing in you so that it can grow.

Amen!

You know, you can have the anointing in a specific field, but it takes fire from the heat of the Holy Spirit to reveal it. The oil alone cannot fry fish! There must be fire to heat it before the fish can be fried. This is similar in the spiritual realm.

This is why it is important for the children of God, to assemble and to put together their anointing, as in upper room, inviting the Holy Spirit to come and fill them. But in the level of protection, a theme that we are currently developing in this chapter, I would like the children of God to understand something very important: everyone has an anointing on their life for protection. This anointing must be constantly heated because we need protection on every day that God has created. Once it is heated, it becomes like a liquid and flows filling all places where we are. That's why wizards cannot stand the anointed presence of God and of people who have an authentic prayer life.

That is why in the prayer programs, an entire environment can become instantly transformed by the presence of God through his servant! Certainly he was anointed from the womb of his mother, but when the Spirit descends on him, automatically the atmosphere of the room or place changes!

There is a real connection between heaven and him, and subsequently between him and the people of God. The Bible says, "It is like precious oil poured on the head, running down on the beard, running down on Aaron's beard, down on the collar of his robe. It is as if the dew of Hermon were falling on Mount Zion. For there the LORD bestows his blessing, even life forevermore." **(Psalm 133:2-3)**

This means that God comes down among His people by His Spirit. It is in this hot oil that there are all sorts of blessings including protection. What did Isaiah say to us? "I saw also the Lord sitting upon a throne, high and lifted up and his train filled the temple." **(Isaiah 6:1)**

At this precise moment where God comes down, the anointing is made available to operate all kinds of miracles. It is left for us to define what we desire as miracle. In Mark, the woman who had the issue of blood for twelve years drew her healing from the robe of Jesus, " And a woman was there who had been subject to bleeding for twelve years. She had suffered a great deal under the care of many doctors and had spent all she had, yet instead of getting better she grew worse. When she heard about Jesus, she came up behind him in the crowd and touched his cloak, because she thought, 'If I just touch his clothes, I will be healed.' Immediately her bleeding stopped and she felt in her body that she was freed from her suffering. At once Jesus realized that power had gone out from him.

He turned around in the crowd and asked, 'Who touched my clothes?'

'You see the people crowding against you,' his disciples answered, 'and yet you can ask, 'Who touched me?'' But Jesus kept looking around to see who had done it. Then the woman, knowing what had happened to her, came and fell at his feet and, trembling with fear, told him the whole truth. He said to her, 'Daughter, your faith has healed you. Go in peace and be freed from your suffering.'" **(Mark 5:25-34)**

Handkerchiefs and cloths that touched the body of Peter were applied to the sick and they were healed and unclean spirits went out of them. It is the Spirit of God that does all these things.

In short, every child of God has an anointing which is specific to him, but we have together the anointing of protection. Activate it by the fire of the Holy Spirit in prayer, because the Spirit dwells in us and lasts forever since Pentecost, "The Spirit of truth. The world cannot accept him, because it neither sees him nor knows him. But you know him, for he lives with you and will be in you." **(John 14:17)**

May God sustain us and help us to understand this mystery in Jesus' Name! Amen! The Holy Spirit is also symbolized by the pillar of cloud. We will not return to the pillar of fire but note that as the pillar of fire was a symbol, the pillar of cloud symbolizes the presence of God in the midst of his children. It was a kind of protection.

Exodus says, "**By day the LORD went ahead of them in a pillar of cloud to guide them on their way and by**

night in a pillar of fire to give them light, so that they could travel by day or night. Neither the pillar of cloud by day nor the pillar of fire by night left its place in front of the people." **(Exodus 13:21-22)**

May the cloud of God guide us wherever we go and may His presence never withdraw from us, Amen!

That the cloud of the Lord ensures our protection during the day and His fire enlightens us during the night is our prayer in the Name of Jesus. This prayer is very important because this is precisely what happened during the crossing of the Red Sea,

"Then the angel of God, who had been traveling in front of Israel's army, withdrew and went behind them. The pillar of cloud also moved from in front and stood behind them, 20 coming between the armies of Egypt and Israel. Throughout the night the cloud brought darkness to the one side and light to the other side; so neither went near the other all night long." (Exodus 14:19-20)

Behold how the Lord extends His hand of protection over His Children. The same cloud split into two, enlightening the children of Israel in their night walk and darkness in the camp of the Egyptians! God did not want the Egyptians to lay their hands on His people so He put himself between the two people.

May the LORD cover our enemies with darkness and enlighten us by His cloud to our promised land, where it flows with milk and honey.

Moreover, outside of the Holy Spirit and His different symbols, God works a lot with the angels as they play an important role in the spiritual warfare and the protection of God's elect.

The Angels of God

God has always sent angels to earth to accomplish different missions. Either they descended to act in favor of the saints by protecting them and fighting at their side, or they came to bring judgment against the enemies of God who walked in rebellion and violated the principles of God the Creator! This means that the presence of the angels can be both a blessing for those who want to be blessed and at the same time fatal for the persecutors who set themselves as the adversaries of the children of God. Their protective role is clearly emphasized by the psalmist, "No harm will overtake you, no disaster will come near your tent. **For He [God] will command his angels concerning you to guard you in all your ways; they will lift you up in their hands,** so that you will not strike your foot against a stone." **(Psalm 91:10-12)** "**The angel of the LORD encamps around those who fear Him,** and He delivers them." **(Psalm 34:7)** As children of God, we have angels around us day and night! And whenever there is a danger, they intervene. They spare us from danger seen and unseen!

Daniel was in danger from ravenous lions because his enemies wanted him dead. But the Lord assured his protection! Listen to him, "**My God sent his angel, and he shut the mouths of the lions. They have not hurt me, because I was found innocent in his sight. Nor have I ever done any wrong before you, Your Majesty.**" **(Daniel**

6:22) The lions could not eat Daniel who was unjustly thrown in their den because God was with him. A single angel was enough to render them harmless. God will send His angel to shut the mouth of the wicked who stalks around you seeking hurt you. I shut the mouth of all the lions that roar against your life, your home, your marriage, your business, and your studies in Jesus' Name and I declare that God's judgment will come against those who wrongly accuse you, as He did for Daniel!

God has not changed; He always protects His children. The same way He sent His angel to shut the lions' mouths is the same way he delivered Apostle Peter in the prison where he was shut up by King Herod. How? By sending an angel! Minimize not the ministry of angels who act on our behalf! Peter was chained and thrown into the depths of the prison where the guards were many. However, God did not need many angels to deliver him despite the fact that he was sleeping between two soldiers with a watchman stationed to guard the door of the prison. "The night before Herod was to bring him to trial, Peter was sleeping between two soldiers, bound with two chains, and sentries stood guard at the entrance. **Suddenly an angel of the Lord appeared** and a light shone in the cell. He struck Peter on the side and woke him up. 'Quick, get up!' he said, and the chains fell off Peter's wrists. Then the angel said to him, 'Put on your clothes and sandals.' And Peter did so. 'Wrap your cloak around you and follow me,' the angel told him. Peter followed him out of the prison, but he had no idea that what the angel was doing was really happening; he thought he was seeing a vision. They passed the first and second guards and came to the iron gate leading to the city. It opened for them by itself, and they went through it. When they had walked the length of one street, **suddenly the angel left him.** Then Peter came to himself and said, 'Now I know without a doubt that the Lord has sent his angel and rescued me from Herod's clutches and from everything the Jewish people were hoping would happen.'" **(Acts 12:6-11)**

God protects His children beyond their thinking! When Syria was at war against Israel, God revealed all their secrets of war and all their plans to Elisha who made it known to the king of Israel. Be coming unbearable, the king of Syria asked his troops to capture the prophet so as to hang him! Elisha was not disturbed and was not afraid, for he knew what was happening spiritually. But his servant who saw the troops exclaimed, "**'Ah! My lord, how shall we do?'** Elisha the prophet, conscious of the protection of God, reassured him and said a prayer, **'Fear not, for those who are with us are more than those who are with them. Elisha prayed, and said, LORD, open his eyes that he may see.'** God responded by answering the prayer of the Prophet, **'And the LORD opened the eyes of the servant, who saw the mountain full of horses and chariots of fire round about Elisha.'"** (2 Kings 6:8-17) In your opinion who are the knights? Are they not the angels of God?

Yes, angels have always been at the service of the children of God. They work to ensure their protection, to strengthen them, to guide them, to inform them, and also to correct according to the mission that God gives them. In

His ministry during His life on earth, even Jesus had need of the ministry of angels. After the devil had tempted him, the angels came to minister to him, "Then the devil left him, **and angels came and attended him**" (Matthew 4:11)

In Gethsemane, He needed the strength of God to face all the trials! In response to his prayer, God sent an angel, "'Father, if you are willing, take this cup from me; yet not my will, but yours be done.' **An angel from heaven appeared to him and strengthened him.**" (Luke 22:42-43)

If Jesus, the Son of God, needed the ministry of angels, we can expect to need them all the more! In addition, it is important to know that angels are formidable! They will not come only to protect and return. No! They also pronounce the judgment of God upon the enemies of the children of God, but under the command and authority of the Lord God!

King Herod maltreated the members of the church when he put James, the brother of John to death by the sword. And again, he had Peter arrested and placed in prison before the angel came to deliver him. This king, because he did not give glory to God in what he was doing, was struck by an angel of the Lord, "On the appointed day Herod, wearing his royal robes, sat on his throne and delivered a public address to the people. They shouted, 'This is the voice of a god, not of a man.' Immediately, because Herod did not give praise to God, **an angel of the Lord struck him down**, and he was eaten by worms and died." (Acts 12:21-23)

Two angels of God were enough to destroy Sodom and Gomorrah, two cities who lived in total abomination;

homosexuality! The people even in their ignorance asked that Lot, who received angels as guests, release them so they can do their dirty work,

"They called to Lot, 'Where are the men who came to you tonight? Bring them out to us so that we can have sex with them.'" **(Genesis 19:5)** The two men said to Lot, "Do you have anyone else here—sons-in-law, sons or daughters, or anyone else in the city who belongs to you? Get them out of here, because we are going to destroy this place. The outcry to the LORD against its people is so great that he has sent us to destroy it." **(Genesis 19:12-13)** "Then the LORD rained down burning sulfur on Sodom and Gomorrah—from the LORD out of the heavens." **(Genesis 19:24)**

Remember, God will always ensure your protection. He never abandons his own! If He protected David in the valley of the shadow of death, He will protect you. If He protected Daniel in the lions' den, He will protect you. If He protected the three Hebrew boys from the fiery furnace, He will protect you. If He protected Joseph from prison to the table of kings, He will protect you. If He protected Mordecai, Esther, and all the Jewish people from the threat of death posed by Haman, he will protect you. If He protected the people from slavery to the Promised Land by passing through the double baptism of the Red Sea and the desert, He will protect you. If He sent angels to minister to Jesus, He will send them to minister to you too. Amen!

He is not your enemy but rather He is your Father!

However, be careful that you do not pray to angels because we do not call upon angels. We pray and call upon the God of the angels and it is He who gives them orders,

"For He will command His angels concerning you to guard you in all your ways;" **(Psalm 91:11)**

"Praise the LORD, you his angels, you mighty ones who do his bidding, who obey his word." **(Psalm 103:20)**

"My God sent his angel, and he shut the mouths of the lions." **(Daniel 6:22)**

"An angel of the Lord struck him down…" **(Acts 12:23)**

"An angel of the Lord appeared" **(Acts 12:7)**

"The angel of the LORD encamps around..." **(Psalm 34:7)**

Angels do not act according to their own will. They listen first, and always to the voice of God before doing anything. Those who acted without His Word are no longer with Him in Heaven; they are called rebellious fallen angels. And they were cast out with the master of the rebellion, Satan, "Its tail swept a third of the stars out of the sky and flung them to the earth.

If you want your prayer answered, call upon God. It is He Who knows which angel or group of angels to send to you on any particular mission. When Sennacherib, king of Assyria had the intention to establish his hegemony in laying hands on all the fortified cities, he sent a letter of threats and insults, not only to the king Hezekiah, but also and especially to the God of Israel. Faced with such a situation, "King Hezekiah and the prophet Isaiah son of Amoz cried out in prayer to heaven about this. And the

LORD sent an angel, who annihilated all the fighting men and the commanders and officers in the camp of the Assyrian king. So he withdrew to his own land in disgrace. And when he went into the temple of his god, some of his sons, his own flesh and blood, cut him down with the sword." **(2 Chronicles 32:20-21)**

Isaiah the prophet tells us the number of the people killed by only one angel, sent by the Lord against Assyria, **"Then the angel of the LORD went out and put to death a hundred and eighty-five thousand in the Assyrian camp. When the people got up the next morning—there were all the dead bodies!" (Isaiah 37:36)**

In Babylonian captivity, Daniel cried out to God, "I prayed to the Lord my God…" **(Daniel 9:4)** and it is God who decided to send him an angel named Gabriel, "While I was still in prayer, Gabriel, the man I had seen in the earlier vision, came to me in swift flight about the time of the evening sacrifice." **(Daniel 9:21)**

Listen carefully to what the angel told Daniel, "As soon as you began to pray, **a word went out**, [where did the word came from? From the mouth of God and as an angel] which I have come to tell you, for you are highly esteemed. Therefore, consider the word and understand the vision" **(Daniel 9:23)**

The angel went to Daniel and instructed: I do not act on my own or on my own will. Likewise, you expect the answer to your prayers the same way. We also expect that the Master of all of us speak before we can deliver the messages. Why? "For you art greatly beloved." This message has been well explained to Apostle John in his revelation by the angel who was sent to him. In fact, the angel asked John to write what he was trying to dictate to him, "And he saith unto me: Write, Blessed are they which are called unto the marriage supper of the Lamb! And he saith unto me: These are the true sayings of God."

John was animated by a spirit of worship when faced with such revelations. He fell at the feet of the angel to worship him, or perhaps just to pray to him or to say thank you... but what is wonderful is that the angel will lead him, like you and me, to the Person; God, "Then the angel said to me, 'Write this: Blessed are those who are invited to the wedding supper of the Lamb!' And he added, 'These are the true words of God.' At this I fell at his feet to worship him. But he said to me, **'Don't do that! I am a fellow servant with you and with your brothers and sisters who hold to the testimony of Jesus.** Worship God! For it is the Spirit of prophecy who bears testimony to Jesus.'" **(Revelation 19:9-10)**

Let the Holy Spirit convince you and do not be distracted. You do not give orders to one that is already subject to authority. We address to the authority, and he gives the green light. Let us turn to God, he will respond positively! However, we specify that if the angel sent by God is present and if he is facing us, God has released him, and he came for us. At that moment, we can speak to him if the opportunity presents itself.

Abraham spoke when he realized he was in front of the angels of God. He interceded on behalf of the city that should be destroyed, because his nephew Lot was there **(Genesis 18)**

In fulfilling their mission when the threat of death was evident, Lot asked the angel to grant him the grace to go, not on the mountain that was far away, but in a small town that was closer. The angel agreed and promised not to destroy the city of refuge of Lot. **(Genesis 19:16-22)**

That said, if you have the grace to receive angels and see them, you can exchange words if their mission permits them. But, if it is to pray for any need or for a special request, contact God directly and make your wishes known to Him.

David, the king of Israel, knew these spiritual realities. Indeed, when he numbered the people of Israel, God was angry against him and his people, so God was about to pronounce a judgment.

70,000 men fell and lose their lives from Dan to Beersheba. David saw the angel whom God had given the order to destroy the people by pestilence. He did not direct words at all to the angel but to God,

David saw the angel that smote the people, but he spoke to the LORD,

"David was conscience-stricken after he had counted the fighting men, and he said to the LORD, "I have sinned greatly in what I have done. Now, LORD, I beg you, take away the guilt of your servant. I have done a very foolish thing." **(2 Samuel 24:10)**

You see, David spoke to God, because the mission of the angel was such that only God could intervene to stop it. The angel continued to execute the order he had received, when another word came out from the mouth of God, **"When the angel stretched out his hand to destroy**

Jerusalem, the LORD relented concerning the disaster and said to the angel who was afflicting the people, 'Enough! Withdraw your hand.'" (2 Samuel 24:16) Then David went to build an altar to offer to God burnt offerings and sacrifices of thanksgiving, "David built an altar to the LORD there and sacrificed burnt offerings and fellowship offerings. Then the LORD answered his prayer in behalf of the land, and the plague on Israel was stopped." **(2 Samuel 24:25)**

Let us remember that it is God who gives orders to His angels. I think we need to have a firm assurance in our God in relation to our protection and His faithfulness.

The Insurance in Spiritual Warfare

Talking about insurance in spiritual warfare requires us to fully trust in the Lord God, as our predecessors in the faith did. Every cloud of fear and doubt must disappear in favor of a shining face full of serenity.

Job reassures us, **"Life will be brighter than noonday, and darkness will become like morning. You will be secure, because there is hope; you will look about you and take your rest in safety." (Job 11:17-18)**

My prayer and my wish are that every child of Jehovah God understands that his Heavenly Father is at his side, to give always the victory. Moses, the great servant of the Lord, reminds us that battle cannot be helped but to take place, but the enemies will always abscond, **"The LORD will grant that the enemies who rise up against you will be defeated before you. They will come at you from one** direction but flee from you in seven." (Deuteronomy 28: 7)

What did prophet Jeremiah tell us? "'**They will fight against you but will not overcome you, for I am with you and will rescue you,' declares the LORD."** (Jeremiah 1:19)

Have faith in God, trust also in Him, and he shall bring it to pass. **(Psalm 37:5)**

Do you know what you mean in the eyes of God?

Abandon ignorance then and embrace knowledge, which is more valuable than all the treasures of the world! **Zechariah 2:8** reveals to us that we are the apple of the eye of the Lord, and consequently, he that touches us, touches the apple of His eye!

Pray this prayer with David and Paul,

"Keep me as the apple of the eye," **(Psalm 17:8)** "Protect my spiritual body with your whole armor, Lord, I am a soldier, put my loins the truth as belt, cover me with the breastplate of righteousness, put as shoes on my feet the readiness that comes from sharing the gospel of peace, give me the shield of faith with which I can quench all the fiery darts of the enemy, put on me the helmet of salvation and give me the sword of the Spirit which is Your word! Amen" **(Ephesians 6:14-17)**

Being in Christ, I want to assure you that no enemy can get to you to harm you, "Your life is hidden with Christ in God." **(Colossians 3:3)** If your life is hidden in Christ, and Christ is hidden in God, I believe you can be fearless and be full of confident like a young lion. He is the one who holds the sword, and decides to fight in order to protect you and make you enter into your prophetic destiny. However, there are many things we need to know. These are actually secrets that are yet to be revealed. That is the revelation of mysteries under the guidance of the Holy Spirit.

Chapter 5:
The Mysteries
Of Spiritual Warfare

There are people who should be in good health, but unfortunately, are sick. There are people who by now should have their own home, but who continue on living with others. There are people who should be feeding their brothers, but still continue to beg for bread. There are people who are supposed to be traveling with their own vehicles but still go about walking.

Do not think that these people do not want to work or that they have 'bad luck'. No! There are mysteries that some of them could not yet transcended. All is not natural, do not forget that man has two bodies. **(1 Corinthians 15:44)**

Allow me to open your eyes to certain realities of spiritual warfare. As you read these lines, there are yokes which will be broken, scales that will fall off from your eyes, and spirits that will be opened with a new strength that will be communicated to you by God. I believe so believe with me and let's go to the Scriptures.

The Mysteries of The Night

The greatest misfortunes that affect human beings are mostly prepared at night, and they only manifest in the day! Indeed, while man sleeps, his enemy came to entreat a covenant with his spirit by sowing evil seed. And when the day appears, he discovers that things are not going well. For nothing, he loses his job, he sees vices been tightening around him and everything becomes difficult, I would say very difficult! Jesus gave us a teaching on this mystery, through the parable of the tares,

"Jesus told them another parable: 'The kingdom of heaven is like a man who sowed **good seed** in his field. But *while everyone was sleeping, his enemy came and sowed weeds among the wheat, and went away.* When the wheat sprouted and formed heads, then the weeds also appeared. The owner's servants came to him and said, 'Sir, didn't you sow good seed in your field? Where then did the weeds come from?'

'An enemy did this,' he replied.

The servants asked him, 'Do you want us to go and pull them up?'" **(Matthew 13:24-28)**

This parable has always been referenced to draw our attention on the last judgment. But apart from this, there is another mystery! The sower sowed "a good seed:

wheat," but when the grass was shifted, what do we find? Another seed distinct from the good 'tares.' Just as the servants of the master, the question is to know when it was done, and who is the author?

Jesus gives us the answer, **"An enemy has done this while people slept."**

In the night, many things happen. It is for this reason that our spirit should be alive (even if the body rests) and be in prayer. The Apostle Peter draws our attention, "Be sober, be vigilant." **(1 Peter 5:8)** One cannot have prayer vigils every day and stay all the time without closing their eyes. Sleep is a biological need. But we have to be awake in the spiritual realm! We must be alive spiritually speaking. The Apostle Paul knows something, "This is why it is said: 'Wake up, sleeper, rise from the dead, and Christ will shine on you.'" **(Ephesians 5:14)**

He who sleeps spiritually is a dead man, because at any time the enemy can make of him what he wants, even to the point of taking his life. But he who is alive, and whose spirit is enlightened by Christ, will escape these powers of darkness. Let's see a little of how the enemy works at night.

As we already mentioned, every divine creature is born with something specific, a grace or a talent that must become a source of joy and happiness for him or her. This thing is received from Heaven and it is God who gives it, "To this John replied, **'A person can receive only what is given them from heaven.'"** **(John 3:27)** But unfortunately, many people have lost what can lead them to success! They live without life!

Clearly, it is during the night that the enemies snatch your gift—your talent that is alive— to give you another that is dead and cannot bring anything to you. A baby who is alive will later become a man. A chick later becomes a rooster or a hen. But a child that is dead, what food are you giving him for him to become a man?

A chick that is not breathing may not be used for anything, because it cannot become a rooster for you to eat or a hen to produce more chicks for you!

In your sleep, there are mysteries! Read this story to understand better, "Now two prostitutes came to the king and stood before him. One of them said, 'Pardon me, my lord. This woman and I live in the same house, and I had a baby while she was there with me. The third day after my child was born, this woman also had a baby. We were alone; there was no one in the house but the two of us. "During the night this woman's son died because she lay on him. **So she got up in the middle of the night and took my son from my side while I your servant was asleep. She put him by her breast and put her dead son by my breast.** The next morning, I got up to nurse my son—and he was dead! But when I looked at him closely in the morning light, I saw that it wasn't the son I had borne.'" **(1 Kings 3:16-21)**

Brother, stop a little at the red light, look at the mirror of your life, and make a retrospect. Think back about yourself and tell me if you are really working in the 'star' that God has given you. Are you really what you are supposed to be? The woman looked 'carefully.' Has something not been replaced?

Do you know that there are parents who work, and shine with the 'star' of their children? Do you know that there are men and women acting with the 'star' of their partner? Yes, there are things and strange practices in the world so you have to put yourself essentially under the cover of God!

My intention is not to shock you, but to wake you up in spiritual warfare. Fight like this prostitute. She fought till she got to the king, and with the divine wisdom granted to Solomon, she was able to take back her living son at the expense of a dead son, "Then the king gave his ruling: **'Give the living baby to the first woman**. Do not kill him; she is his mother.'" **(1 Kings 3:27)** I prophesy that you possess your living child, and your shining 'Star' in the Name of Jesus. Amen!

This woman struggled when she realized that something happened during the night and her living son was removed in replacement of the dead son belonging to another prostitute! She made a return-to-sender and took back what belonged to her.

Take back what has been stolen and live your life according to the plan of God.

It is always at night that the devil incites to sin, "They called to Lot, 'Where are the men who came to you tonight? Bring them out to us so that we can have sex with them.'" **(Genesis 19:5)** The inhabitants of Sodom wanted during the night to sodomize the angels that God sent. In this same way, the prince of darkness leads those whose spirit is under his control, in abominable and indescribable things. Is it not at night that the devil prepares the fall of the shepherds, the men of God in order to scatter the sheep of the Lord?

Jesus spoke of this mystery in Matthew, "Then Jesus told them, 'This very night you will all fall away on account of me, for it is written: 'I will strike the shepherd, and the sheep of the flock will be scattered.'"" **(Matthew 26:31)** That same night, Jesus was arrested, "So Judas came to the garden, guiding a detachment of soldiers and some officials from the chief priests and the Pharisees. They were carrying torches, lanterns and weapons." **(John 18:3)**

"Then seizing him, they led him away and took him into the house of the high priest. Peter followed at a distance. And when some there had kindled a fire in the middle of the courtyard and had sat down together, Peter sat down with them." **(Luke 22:54-55)**

They put on the fire because it was simply night!

The Apostle Paul adds, "The Lord Jesus, on **the night he was betrayed...**" **(1 Corinthians 11:23)** It was in the night that Jesus was arrested! And it is he who knew him very well, that Satan used to deliver him that night. And how? With a kiss! "While he was still speaking a crowd came up, and the man who was called Judas, one of the Twelve, was leading them. He approached Jesus to kiss him, but Jesus asked him, 'Judas, are you betraying the Son of Man with a kiss?'" **(Luke 22:47-48)**

As soon as Jesus was arrested, the disciples scattered, "Then everyone deserted him and fled." **(Mark 14:50)** The only one that held on in all these ended up denying him,

"Then Peter remembered the word Jesus had spoken: 'Before the rooster crows, you will disown me three times.' And he went outside and wept bitterly." **(Matthew 26:75)**

The wicked could say at this point that he has achieved his objectives; arrest the shepherd and scatter the disciples. But Jesus has said, "This is your hour and the power of darkness." **(Luke 22:53 King James Version)**

The night is their best time. It is for us to wake up in prayer. This is the time to remind the members that they should pray for their shepherds. Paul asked, "As for other matters, brothers and sisters, pray for us that the message of the Lord may spread rapidly and be honored, just as it was with you. And pray that we may be delivered from wicked and evil people, for not everyone has faith." **(2 Thessalonians 3:1-2 NIV)**

However, apart from the anointed of God, Satan can take the image of people we know or are familiar with, to destroy us in spiritual warfare. Judas was well known to Jesus, but he delivered him to his captors. In the night, a spirit can come to do you evil and if you are awake in the spirit and at the point that you are battle ready, he takes the face of a brother or a parent. Then you refuse to continue the battle because you do not want to hurt a member of your family! No, you must continue the battle, even if you wake up, continue the battle in prayer. Remember, it is not the person you are fighting, but the spirit. If you relax, he will come back another time. Destroy him in the name of Jesus.

For example, the case of a spiritual husband or wife. They take very often the faces we know, to have intimacy with us. This is the trick of the devil! Reject it in Jesus' Name.

Also, the spirit of death is very comfortable at night. Either he kills outright the person at night, or he puts everything in place for the person to die the following day. It is in the night that witches that I can call 'the soul eaters' perform their dirtiest works. The son of the prostitute died during the night as his mother laid on him. **(1Kings 3:19)**

To afflict the Egyptians with the death of the firstborn concerning their rebellion against God, it happened during the night, "At midnight the LORD **struck down all the firstborn in Egypt,** from the firstborn of Pharaoh, who sat on the throne, to the firstborn of the prisoner, who was in the dungeon, and the firstborn of all the livestock as well. Pharaoh and all his officials and all the Egyptians got up *during the night*, and there was loud wailing in Egypt, for there was not a house without someone dead." **(Exodus 12:29-30)**

At what time of the day did God promise to snatch the soul of the rich fool? "But God said to him, 'You fool! This very night your life will be demanded from you. Then who will get what you have prepared for yourself?'" **(Luke 12:20)**

In short, this is one of the reasons why God wakes us up some nights so that we remain in His presence, and especially using one of our weapons! Either we remain in prayer, meditation, or in worship. When the enemy comes as we sleep to entreat a covenant with our spirit, he comes in order to hurt us, make us sick, impoverish us, or take our very lives. Our heavenly guardian touches us so that we can destroy and put off their work. Staying in the presence of God a few hours at night makes us strong during the day! It is not in vain that we organize prayer vigils. We should attack the enemy during the night!

Abram, our father in faith, gives us an example to follow. Indeed, when his brother was taken captive, he went to deliver him attacking in the night, "When Abram heard that his relative had been taken captive, he called out the 318 trained men born in his household and went in pursuit as far as Dan. During the night Abram divided his men to attack them and he routed them, pursuing them as far as Hobah, north of Damascus. He recovered all the goods and brought back his relative Lot and his possessions, together with the women and the other people." **(Genesis 14:14-16)**

If we can attack at night, we will get back everything that was taken or snatched from us, Amen!

The enemy is obliged to liberate our soul or our property if we bombard him with our sophisticated and powerful weapons by virtue of God. When God bombarded the Egyptians, in the same night, Pharaoh allowed Israel to go after much resistance and obstinacy, "During the night Pharaoh summoned Moses and Aaron and said, 'Up! Leave my people, you and the Israelites! Go, worship the LORD as you have requested.'" **(Exodus 12:31)** "The Egyptians urged the people to hurry and leave the country. 'For otherwise,' they said, 'we will all die!'" **(Exodus 12:33)**

Whatever time it will take, do not give up in prayer, instead, continue as Moses did. Your enemy must recognize that you have a God. Pharaoh did not recognize the God of the Hebrews. He even said: who is the LORD that I should let you go?

But when the night battle took place, he acknowledged that Israel had a God that they need to go and worship, "Go, serve the LORD as you have said." Your physical or spiritual enemy must get here through your night prayers.

Do you know that there are spiritual entities that you should snatch, kill, ruin, and destroy before building another altar to the LORD, and during the night! This is the message that God sent to Gideon, "And it came to pass the same night that the LORD said unto him, take your father's young bullock, even the second bullock of seven years old and throw down the altar of Baal that your father hath, and cut down the grove that is by it. And build an altar unto the Lord your God upon the top of this rock, in the ordered place, and take the second bullock, and offer a burnt sacrifice with the wood of the groove which you will cut down."

Gideon took advantage of the mystery that God revealed to him:

He had to begin by destroying all that prevented the glory of God before the battle against the Midianites that oppressed them. He will obey and do what God told him, "Then Gideon took ten men of his servants and did as the LORD had said unto him, **he executed in the night and not in the day.**" **(Judges 6:25-27 KJV)**

The people of the city who did not have the revelation of what God told him, could have been obstacles to the accomplishment of these things. But as he did everything in the night, they were surprised in the morning of the next day!

Destroy the altar of Baal that prevents the hand of God to move in your family and cut down the sacred pole in the name of Jesus! Build another altar of praise, worship, prayer and meditation, and the glory of the Lord will appear to the surprise of everyone! Amen!

The strength of the great men of God emanates from their relationship with God during the hours of the night. Jesus certainly taught during the day and prayed in the night, **"Each day Jesus was teaching at the temple, and each evening he went out to spend the night on the hill called the Mount of Olives,** and all the people came early in the morning to hear him at the temple." **(Luke 21:37-38 NIV)**

Why? There was simply power in His Word which was different from that of the scribes. Listening to him, the people were edified, "When Jesus had finished saying these things, the crowds were amazed at his teaching, because he taught as one who had authority, and not as their teachers of the law." **(Matthew 7:28-29)**

God does not care about the darkness, what interests him is the light! So, in the same way He spoke, speak also, declare light on the thick darkness of your life. Call upon the name of Jesus. It is Him, the Light, that makes the prince of darkness to flee. Light and darkness cannot coexist. Where there is light, darkness will pack its bags. Your night is hectic, you cannot sleep, and you feel a strange heaviness that you do not understand? Does your spirit seem to be away from your body? Kneel down, call upon the name of Jesus, and you will see the result. What does John say? "When Jesus spoke again to the people, he said, 'I am the light of the world. Whoever follows me will never walk in darkness, but will have the light of life.'" **(John 8:12)**

I pray that Christ will be the light of our lives today and forever! Amen! In these mysteries of the night, God in His grace takes time to reveal himself to us, in order to draw our attention to the realities of the spiritual world. He opens the window and removes the veil and that, through dreams.

The Mysteries of Dreams

The Book of the Prophet Jeremiah says, "Call to me and I will answer you and tell you great and unsearchable things you do not know." **(Jeremiah 33:3)**

David could also prophesy, "I will instruct you and teach you in the way you should go; I will counsel you with my loving eye on you." **(Psalm 32:8)** These are the words of Lord in the mouth of His servants. This implies that God speaks and reveals mysteries that the Holy Scriptures calls the great things; the hidden things. In effect, He announces it in different ways through His Word, by the circumstances of life, and by dreams and visions of the night. The only problem is that despite God removing the veil to talk to us, man cannot perceive the mysteries that lie behind these revelations. Job supports this truth, "For God does speak—now one way, now another— though no one perceives it. In a dream, in a vision of the night, when deep sleep falls on people as they slumber in their beds," **(Job 33:14-15)**

Do not forget God does nothing for nothing; everything He does is for precise and specific purpose. And he decided to speak to us through dreams and visions of the night; it is for something good.

Father God loves us and his love extends to all children even if they do not recognize Him as Father. By dreams, God warns us of things to come so that we take necessary precaution and on time. God is Omniscient. He knows everything, so He gives us information. The information is for us to be wise and to use wisely.

Pharaoh, a pagan king, had a dream, "When two full years had passed, Pharaoh had a dream: He was standing by the Nile, when out of the river there came up seven cows, sleek and fat, and they grazed among the reeds. After them, seven other cows, ugly and gaunt, came up out of the Nile and stood beside those on the riverbank. And the cows that were ugly and gaunt ate up the seven sleek, fat cows. Then Pharaoh woke up. He fell asleep again and had a second dream: Seven heads of grain, healthy and good, were growing on a single stalk. After them, seven other heads of grain sprouted—thin and scorched by the east wind. The thin heads of grain swallowed up the seven healthy, full heads. Then Pharaoh woke up; it had been a dream." **(Genesis 41:1-7)**

God spoke to him in a dream that the two things would happen in the fourteen years that follow! He had no explanation, but he knew effectively in his mind that there was a mystery behind his dream! It was for this reason that he called all the magicians and all the other wise men of Egypt to explain this mystery to him. They would not succeed in doing so because it came from God and can only be explained by one that has been filled with the Spirit of God, "The LORD confides in those who fear him; he makes his covenant known to them." **(Psalm 25:14)**

Thus Joseph, a young Hebrew that had the fear of God and was thrown in prison because of the lie of the wife of his master Potiphar, came out through the channel of the cupbearer to the king that he gave an explanation of his dream while they were in the same prison cell.

Joseph is going to tell the king Pharaoh that the two dreams convey the same message. There will indeed be seven years of plenty, symbolized by the seven good cows, and the seven good ears and seven more years of famine and starvation represented by seven cows ugly and gaunt and the seven empty ears and burned.

To avoid starvation, he should begin collecting part of the crop to put in stores. And these are stocks that would feed the people during the years of drought and famine. King Pharaoh acted accordingly and was not surprised! For what Joseph explained, happened exactly.

You know there are situations that you can avoid or you can escape from if and only if you allow yourself to be warned through dreams that God gives you. That implies that God teaches us in dreams. It becomes our responsibility to follow or reject His instructions. He does not force anyone!

When Jesus was in Bethlehem in Judea, the Bible says that Wise men from the East came to Jerusalem to worship

Him. Their worship was sincere. With their wisdom, they had the ability to read the messages conveyed by the stars. The star that shone as soon as Jesus was born could not allow them to be indifferent; they had to come and bow before this child because his star revealed that he was King,

"…Where is the one who has been born king of the Jews? We saw his star when it rose and have come to worship him." **(Matthew 2:2)**

But King Herod and all of Jerusalem were troubled! After information from the chief priests and scribes of the people, Herod would go back to the Wise men with the idea of going too, once they had returned from their voyage to adore the Child Jesus, "He sent them to Bethlehem and said, 'Go and search carefully for the child. As soon as you find him, report to me, so that I too may go and worship him.'" **(Matthew 2:8)**

Without explanation, our Omniscient God, warned the Wise Men that they were not to return to Herod. They followed His instructions, "And **having been warned in a dream** not to go back to Herod, they returned to their country by another route." **(Matthew 2:12)**

We bless God for the wisdom of the wise men, otherwise what would have happened if they had refused to obey the divine instructions received during their sleep in a dream? The intention of Herod will be revealed to Joseph in a dream also. And there, God gives instructions to thwart his plans, "When they had gone, an angel of the Lord appeared to Joseph in a dream. 'Get up,' he said, 'take the child and his mother and escape to Egypt. Stay there until I tell you, for Herod is going to search for the child to kill him.'" **(Matthew 2:13)**

The fiancé of Mary, the mother of Jesus, did not downplay the revelation and did not say that it is a simple dream! He reacted automatically bending to the will of God, "So he [Joseph] got up, took the child and his mother during the **night** and left for Egypt," **(Matthew 2:14)** And thanks to his obedience, the worst was avoided! Glory be to God!

Also in the Old Testament, there is a man who, despite his weaknesses, knew the importance of dreams in spiritual warfare. He was called Balaam. Indeed, our God swore to Abraham, Isaac, and Jacob to bless them and their offspring. It happened by a covenant in which Abraham secured the blessing of his offspring and subsequently secure and protect his descendant. Indeed, God asked Abraham to offer his son Isaac as a burnt offering in the land of Moriah on one of the mountains indicated. It is on this mountain that Yahweh-God would establish his covenant with the one we called the father of faith. Because he accepted, despite what it might cost him, to offer his only son. The angel of the Lord intervened and the child was spared, but the miracle of the covenant is in the submission of Abraham to the word of his Heavenly Father! Listen to words pronounced on Abraham and by extension on the fruits of his womb, "and said, "I swear by myself, declares the LORD, that because you have done this and have not withheld your son, your only son, I will surely bless you and make your descendants as numerous as the stars in the sky and as the sand on the seashore.

Your descendants will take possession of the cities of their enemies," **(Genesis 22:16-17)**

In short, it is blessed people of God that king Balak wanted to curse and chase away from his territory because he greatly feared the people of Israel. But his mistake was that he wanted to curse Israel on behalf of the God of Israel, who anointed the person to whom he has called Balaam. When the elders of Moab and Midian came to him, he asked one thing, "'Spend the **night** here,' Balaam said to them, 'and I will report back to you with the answer the LORD gives me.' So the Moabite officials stayed with him." **(Numbers 22:8)**

This anointed of God knew the mysteries of the night and the mysteries of night revelations! Moreover, God can never contradict himself. He told his servant Balaam not to go with them, giving him the reasons for his refusal, "But God said to Balaam, 'Do not go with them. **You must not put a curse on those people**, because they are blessed.'" **(Numbers 22:12)**

Brothers and sisters, do the things that will move God to make covenant with us! Because he can change a promise or a prophecy, but his covenant is eternal! Despite all that the Jewish people did, despite their disobedience in many ways, despite their feeling like the forsaken of God, — sometimes to other gods— the Lord remained faithful to his covenant forged with Abraham. There is a force in the covenant of the Lord! He can certainly punish in case of disobedience, but his covenant remains. Hallelujah! That is what is wonderful!

Moreover, after the refusal of Balaam, Balak sent other leaders considered more influential than the first group. The approach of Balaam did not change. He wished to receive instructions from God during the night, before engaging in anything, "But Balaam answered them, 'Even if Balak gave me all the silver and gold in his palace, I could not do anything great or small to go beyond the command of the LORD my God [as if to say that He that has anointed me and it is impossible to curse a people whom He has declared blessed]. Now spend the night here so that I can find out what else the LORD will tell me.'" **(Numbers 22:18-19)**

Since God knew everything that would happen and what He would do, He finished by permitting Balaam to go with them. Along the way, God sent an angel with a drawn sword in his hand. He opened the mouth of the donkey that spoke as a man. He opens the eyes of Balaam to see the angel that asks him to bend to the will of God. The angel tells him what God expects him to say. And repeating to him not to be allowed to be influenced by the weight and value of the gifts of the King of Moab. The rest of the story tells us that the people of Moab, including King Balak had provided everything needed including: seven altars, seven bulls and seven rams, three times, and in three different places.

And from these different places, God still blessed his people through the mouth of his servant Balaam. This is what God asked him to do when he received the princes of Moab. He received orders of the night and followed!

We must do the same.

In addition, in dreams and visions, God reveals himself to us to preserve us from pride. You know that God hates pride, "That is why Scripture says: 'God opposes the proud but shows favor to the humble.'" **(James 4:6)**

One might ask how does He resist the proud?

Isaiah the prophet gives us the answer, "The eyes of the arrogant will be humbled and human pride brought low; the LORD alone will be exalted in that day. The LORD Almighty has a day in store for all the proud and lofty, for all that is exalted (and they will be humbled)," **(Isaiah 2:11-12)**

This is what happened to Lucifer! He was lowered and cast down to serve as an example to us. It is for this reason that God puts us on guard against pride. He takes time to speak to us through images and dreams! He did it with King Nebuchadnezzar.

God has indeed spoken many times and in many ways, to this powerful Babylonian king, but he was not ready for advice; unlike the Egyptian king. Let's see his dream and what happened to him,

"These are the visions I saw while lying in bed: I looked, and there before me stood a tree in the middle of the land. Its height was enormous. The tree grew large and strong and its top touched the sky; it was visible to the ends of the earth. Its leaves were beautiful, its fruit abundant, and on it was food for all. Under it the wild animals found shelter, and the birds lived in its branches; from it every creature was fed. In the visions I saw while lying in bed, I looked, and there before me was a holy one, a messenger, coming down from heaven. He called in a loud voice: 'Cut down the tree and trim off its branches; strip off its leaves and scatter its fruit. Let the animals flee from under it and the birds from its branches. But let the stump and its roots, bound with iron and bronze, remain in the ground, in the grass of the field. Let him be drenched with the dew of heaven, and let him live with the animals among the plants of the earth. **Let his mind be changed from that of a man and let him be given the mind of an animal**, till seven times pass by for him. The decision is announced by messengers, the holy ones declare the verdict, so that the living may know that the Most High is sovereign over all kingdoms on earth and gives them to anyone he wishes and sets over them the lowliest of people.' This is the dream that I, King Nebuchadnezzar, had. Now, Belteshazzar, tell me what it means, for none of the wise men in my kingdom can interpret it for me. But you can, because the spirit of the holy gods is in you." **(Daniel 4:10-18)**

May God spare us such a dream!

The big tree was the king himself, a man to whom God had given power and authority. But now it will be removed according to the explanation of Daniel, the Prophet, "You will be driven away from people and will live with the wild animals; you will eat grass like the ox and be drenched with the dew of heaven. Seven times will pass by for you until you acknowledge that the Most High is sovereign over all kingdoms on earth and gives them to anyone he wishes." **(Daniel 4:25)**

Daniel took the opportunity to counsel him; to put an end to his sins and his iniquities by practicing righteousness **(Daniel 4:27)** "There is no one that is deafer than he who refuses to listen."

The king would continue in his pride. He said, 'Is not this the great Babylon **I have built** as the royal residence, by **my mighty power** and for the glory of **my majesty**?'" **(Daniel 4:30)**

While he was still speaking, a voice came down from heaven to repeat the same words that the prophet Daniel had said to him, "You will be driven away from people and will live with the wild animals; you will eat grass like the ox and be drenched with the dew of heaven. Seven times will pass by for you until you acknowledge that the Most High is sovereign over all kingdoms on earth and gives them to anyone he wishes." **(Daniel 4:25)**

His dream was fulfilled, despite the opportunity he had to stop and humble himself before God. But what is interesting and wonderful is that Nebuchadnezzar was broken and the lesson given by God stuck in his mind. Listen to some of these edifying words coming from someone who had lived in pride but was reshaped by God,

"At the end of that time, **I, Nebuchadnezzar, raised my eyes toward heaven, and my sanity was restored. Then I praised the Most-High; I honored and glorified him who lives forever. His dominion is an eternal dominion; his kingdom endures from generation to generation.** All the peoples of the earth are regarded as nothing. He does as he pleases with the powers of heaven and the peoples of the earth. No one can hold back his hand or say to him: "What have you done?" At the same time that my sanity was restored, my honor and splendor were returned to me for the glory of my kingdom. My advisers and nobles sought me out, and I was restored to my throne and became even greater than before. **Now I, Nebuchadnezzar, praise and exalt and glorify the King of heaven, because everything he does is right and all his ways are just. And those who walk in pride he is able to humble." (Daniel 4:34-37)**

Praise God for this man, who had the time to repent, and who recognized the hand of God in the kingdom of men. Let us draw inspiration from the mistakes of others to avoid the punishment that they endured. There is also outside of what we have seen (the dreams we have from God) to reveal to us that the enemy is preparing against us. And to protect our soul from the pit; our life from the blows of the sword.

All these things are well explained by Job, "For God does speak—now one way, now another— though no one perceives it. In a dream, in a vision of the night, when deep sleep falls on people as they slumber in their beds," **(Job 33:14-15)** But why does God speak this way? Job continues, **"He may speak in their ears and terrify them with warnings, to turn them from wrongdoing and keep them from pride, to preserve them from the pit, their lives from perishing by the sword." (Job 33:16-18)**

God is not pleased with our premature death. He wants us to live long! To die in the prime of life is certainly not His desire for His beloved children which we are, even if it happens unfortunately sometimes. Which fathers of this world wish to bury any of their children? Is it not our prayer to see our children grow and bury us with dignity when death will take us!

Jesus tells us that if we, who are wicked, know how to give good things to our children, how much more our heavenly father will give unto us even wonderful things. **(Matthew 7:11)**

Listen to what God promises His child that you are, His child that I am, "With long life I will satisfy him and show him my salvation." **(Psalm 91:16)**

This promise is for all the children of God, wherever they are found. And if they are aware of this, God will never refuse to reveal secrets to them nor to save them from death if they ask him. This is what happened in Babylon when King Nebuchadnezzar had his first dream. He indeed called on all his magicians, astrologers, wise men and Chaldeans (priests or educated people) for them to find the dream that had eluded him Once they found the dream, they would give him the explanation; that was impossible! The immediate consequence was a death sentence issued by the king, who was angry and became very hysterical! Faced with such a situation, Daniel and his Hebrew companions, all captives of the king, were not spared. They were part of the wise men of Babylon. Daniel, by divine wisdom and prudent manner, spoke to the commander of the king, Arioch, who would lead him to the king. He pleaded for some time to explain the king's dream. The grace of God could not but manifest before such a situation. So, the king accepted the request of the young Hebrew! But the death sentence was still there, he had to at all costs to know the dream before he could explain.

Daniel knew the promises of God,

"And call on me in the day of trouble; I will deliver you, and you will honor me." **(Psalm 50:15)**

"I will instruct you and teach you in the way you should go; I will counsel you with my loving eye on you." **(Psalm 32:8)**

"The righteous person may have many troubles, but the LORD delivers him from them all;" **(Psalm 34:19)**

"'They will fight against you but will not overcome you, for I am with you and will rescue you,' declares the LORD." **(Jeremiah 1:19)**

"Do not be anxious about anything, but in every situation, by prayer and petition, with thanksgiving, present your requests to God." **(Philippians 4:6)**

"For no word from God will ever fail." **(Luke 1:37)**

"He urged them to plead for mercy from the God of heaven concerning this mystery, so that he and his friends might not be executed with the rest of the wise men of Babylon." **(Daniel 2:18)**

Glory be to God for, "During the night the mystery was revealed to Daniel in a vision. Then Daniel praised the God of heaven." **(Daniel 2:19)**

This is how God revealed himself to Daniel; to spare him from a sudden death and out of His plan.

Brother, what do you know about the dreams that you receive? There are dreams or night visions that God gives you specifically to wake you up from sleep, so you may engage in a real spiritual warfare, intense prayer, a consecration to God, or total surrender to God! The enemy roars, intending to devour! And you, what do you do?

Let us see the meaning of some dreams:

Bad Dreams

• If you stumble or you climb a mountain and you slide to the bottom or you always come down from a lift, a ladder, or stairs, you have to quickly get into fasting and in prayer and potentially even go see a man of God for deliverance! The enemy wants you to stumble in your work, in your studies, or in your business. His intention is that you do not accomplish what you are doing. Clearly, they want you to have a dramatic fall; it is a spirit of failure and blockage that are positioning themselves in front of you. This is the same for he who, in his dream, takes a dead-end road or sees that a tree is blocking his way. Pray with **Deuteronomy 28:13**.

• If you're sitting on a chair or on a rocker comfortably, and they make you stand up without giving you another chair or another rocker, be careful to rebuke the spirit of joblessness! They want to take your source of income. Battle with the name of Jesus. But, if after they took your chair, they give you a less comfortable one, it is that they want you to regress; Pray against demotion. You have to get up the same night and stand on your feet. Do not remain in bed Do not give the time for this project to come to pass. Pray and destroy it through the power in the name of Jesus!

• There are some people with whom we work who are against our promotion or what we want. They engage in evil practices or visit witch doctors, diviners, and others. And God reveals to us while they are doing it in a symbolic or pictorial way.

At the same time, we must kill this chick in the egg. We must destroy their bomb in their hands. Send the bomb of the Holy Spirit or the Blood of Jesus in their camp and arsenal to destroy all in the name of Jesus!

• If you have a dream where you are given a snail or if you are gathering either a snail or tortoise - if you're on a wet road and moreover slippery, arise and fight against every spirit of delay! You are likely to be behind in everything you do and in your life. Pray and rebuke delay, breaking the spirit in the name of Jesus. Declare your success as soon as possible by the power of the Holy Spirit.

• It is the same thing for someone who has a habit of eating in his dream. The meal you eat weighs you down in spirit. It will be difficult for you to surface as everything will be slow. It is as if they sent you a spirit of slumber. After a good meal, we may feel sleepy. Brother, get up and pray. This can also be a spiritual spell to make you sick or poison your blood! Pray with **Psalm 3**!

• But if you eat meat or a meal in a dream, if you go hunting with people to kill animals, or you cut meat and prepare it; you are already a wizard or you are being initiated. Join a prayer camp or retreat center to confide in a man of God otherwise you will begin delivering your parents consciously or unconsciously. For what you eat is the parents of others; in your turn, your creditors will claim yours! If you had such dreams, get up immediately and pray. Say, "I refuse to be sorcerer in Jesus' Name! I reject any introduction or initiation to witchcraft in the name of Jesus. I called the Blood of Jesus and I declare that you are defeated. I send the fire of the Holy Spirit to consume the debris of this covenant in the name of Jesus. I will never be a sorcerer, but instead I will serve Jesus Christ and I will be a blessing to others." **(Deuteronomy 27:7; Joshua 10:8)**

• If they shoot you in a dream or a dog, cat, snake, lion, or tiger bites or claws you… If you are pursued by cattle or pigs, or if you see a masquerade pursuing you or an owl… If you see soldiers, police, and others pursuing you or if you are in the middle of a group of people, brother or sister, sorcerers are chasing you. They want you to be sick so you may spend all your money, risk your peace of mind, or be killed. **(John 10:10)**

If you had these kind of dreams, you do not have a right to be far away from God. You must instead hold fast to Him with all your strength.

If in your dream, you see your blood flowing because you are shot or because you were bitten or scratched by an animal, pray and say, "I am a child of God and the blood of Jesus was shed for me. I neutralize the power of the venom and the bite, in Jesus' name and all your plans are doomed to failure. You who pursue me, I scatter you, I mix up your language, I have turned you back-against-back and I confuse your language as God did at the tower of Babel **(Genesis 11:1-9)** You soldiers of the devil who are pursuing me, know I stand in the Blood of Jesus and declare that you have come through one way, but you shall scatter by seven ways for the LORD is with me like a Hero warrior." **(Deuteronomy 28:7; Jeremiah 20:11)**

• When you see a bird in a cage or taken in a net, or a sheep attached somewhere, your soul is in danger. It is of the fowlers or spiritual predators who seek to devour you. Pray the same prayer as before and add, "I declare that I come out of your net, your spiritual fowlers, you are overcome by the Blood of Jesus. I tear the net with the sword of the Word of God and I am free in the Name of Jesus **(Psalm 91:3)** Anyone you have tied to make a game is released in the name of Jesus. I loose all the snares that you have made, I declare that the rope is broken and the soul returns to the body in the name of Jesus. May the Spirit of the Lord disperse you in the Name of Jesus!" **(Isaiah 59:19)**

• If you are used to seeing a relative who has died in a dream, or if you constantly see a coffin or a funeral, or if you find yourself in mourning dress, the spirit of death is not far away. It could be you or a person you are close to that has been threatened with death. You must automatically rise up to destroy any spirit of death whatever its origin. Say, "I break the coffin by the power of the Holy Spirit in Jesus' Name. I refuse all premature burial for me or any of my relatives in the name of Jesus. You, roaring spirit of death, remain where you are. A dead relative cannot come back **(Isaiah 26:14, Job 7:9)** you're a liar and you are overcome by the Blood of Jesus.

I declare long life on me and on my relatives in the name of Jesus **(Psalm 91:16)** I declare that I shall not die, but live and also my relatives (husband, wife, children, brothers and sisters) We shall testify to the works of the Lord in Jesus' name." **(Psalm 118:17)**

• In your dream, if you see a car accident or if you see blood flowing on the road, the enemy has planned an accident to drink blood. Human blood has power in the spiritual world. It is what the devil and his demons drink; even wizards. This makes them even more terrible!

This is why you often see accidents which follow one after the other. Be careful, there are accidents programmed from the spiritual world, and this is what we are talking about! Sometimes the driver sees a tree or a big stone in the middle of the road and wanting to avoid it, manages a "senseless" accident; this is a program! Sometimes they bind the soul of someone to a car to find a reason to justify his death. A person wants to cross the road and, seeing there is no danger, decides to make an attempt. But the moment he engages, Bam!

His blood leaves his body and death follows soon afterward. These are the things that are hidden that are being prepared, that your God has shown you, you must get up to instantly and destroy it!

Your prayer will be of great efficacy because behind all divine revelation, there is a special anointing to break the yoke. **(Isaiah 10:27)**

Amen!

Stand on your feet lest you sleep and start praying,

"I destroy all bridges and all spiritual check points you have installed to cause accidents. I stand in the Blood of Jesus and I declare that your projects of accident, death, and the flowing of blood will not come to pass in the name of Jesus. The power of the Holy Spirit will blow away all the bridges and check points so cars move normally in the name of Jesus. I declare that I will not die by accident, neither my relatives nor any child of God who is on your list in the Name of Jesus!"

• If you see the wind blowing hard, you could be about to go through difficult times. It is the image of the great trials like the wind that killed Job's children!

• If you see a crazy man pursuing you, they are the evil spirits. They do not have the right. Pray with **Psalm 27**.

• If in your dream you are picking up needles, or if you are sitting on the toilet, it is the spirit of chronic poverty. Quote **Haggai 2:8** and pray with **Proverbs 10:22**. Refuse it with violence.

• Cut hair in a dream is a curse because it represents the glory, especially for women!

• Being intoxicated from drinking alcohol is the difficulty of life. Refuse negative spiritual drunkenness.

• Removed clothes, being naked or a removed tooth in a dream represents shame; the opposite of glory. You must be careful concerning everything you do; otherwise you run the risk of being in confusion and in shame.

In short, there are dreams and dreams... we cannot finish to quote them. One thing is certain, as soon as you have a bad dream, know that it is God who is warning you about the counsels of the wicked; it is your responsibility to pray. Do you have any dreams where spirits sleep with you taking the face of people you know, rise up and destroy the seeds they put in you or take back the seed they have extracted from your body, according to your sex. It is in the spiritual erotic scenes that the enemy often snatches our fertility giving us all kinds of diseases (Cysts, fibroids, epilepsy, menstrual pain, loss of blood, impotence...) You must always pray until they stop sleeping with you in your dreams. Close the doors and windows through which they come into your life through prayer and by the Blood of Jesus. Do you have dreams where you always find yourself in the water? Seek your deliverance otherwise a water spirit will make you move from man-to-man without being able to be satisfied and you will not be able to marry. It is the same case with men. Everyone may desire you, but nobody would decide to marry you. It is the job of the water spirit with her boss the queen of heaven who hates marriage.

May the Lord deliver us and help us to understand these mysteries as well as the good dreams that He gives us. Amen!

Good Dreams

About good dreams, we must say that we have one way or the other touch it. These are the dreams that God gives to warn us in respect of our future or our tomorrow. He also reveals straightly who we are! To have this kind of dream, we must pray before going to sleep and ask God to reveal himself to us.

• Being baptized in a dream means that one must live a life of sanctification through repentance, sin must die in us. It's the same for a person who sees himself in a white tunic. God wants you to live a life according to His Word. **(Ecclesiastes 9:8)**

• Meeting an authority in a dream is a good thing, it is a sign of a future elevation according to the stature of the authority seen in the spiritual world.

• Harvesting of cereals such as wheat, millet, rice or cutting a bunch of plantains, bananas, or sweet potatoes, even uprooting yam tubers means that your business will work and there will be a good influx of money. When the bananas are ripe know that it will not delay; you should simply continue praying **(Isaiah 55:10-11)** and monitor what you do.

• When in your dream you are in the rain understand that you are financially blessed by God, and you will be rich.

• If several people greet you by shaking your hand, it is a congratulation. You will live a great time!

• If you happen to catch a lot of birds in your dream, by intelligence, you will defeat your enemies; foiling their traps **(Proverbs 16:7)**

• If you see yourself preaching, it means that you are a preacher and God has deposited this anointing on your life, speak of Jesus around you and preach the Word of God.

• If you see yourself fishing or catching fish, you are a soul winner for the Kingdom of God. From your efforts, God will snatch men from the devil's hand and lead them in His kingdom.

Jesus said to Simon Peter, who was with his brother Andrew,

"'Come, follow me,' Jesus said, 'and I will send you out to fish for people.'" **(Matthew 4:19)**

• If you are doing deliverance in your dream, know God is calling you to the ministry. You can be in a church or with a man of God, and when the spirits manifest, you have to join in prayer to continue the deliverance of the people following them until they are completely free!

• There are men who are born to be 'great'; to be leaders, pace-setters, and to lead others. This grace was given to them from Heaven and God reveals this in a dream, using signs like the sun and the stars. This was the case of Joseph. Remember his dreams, "Joseph had a dream, and when he told it to his brothers, they hated him all the more. He said to them, 'Listen to this dream I had: We were binding sheaves of grain out in the field when suddenly my sheaf rose and stood upright, while your sheaves gathered around mine and bowed down to it.' His brothers said to him, 'Do you intend to reign over us? Will you actually rule us?' And they hated him all the more because of his dream and what he had said. Then he had another dream, and he told it to his brothers. 'Listen,' he said, 'I had another dream, and this time the sun and moon and eleven stars were bowing down to me.'"
(Genesis 37:5-9)

These dreams are clear and show that Joseph, who seems to be the smallest, is actually the greatest! He must "command" by the power that God has given him. His father was represented by the sun, and his mother was symbolized by the moon. The eleven other brothers were the image of eleven stars! God showed him the dream twice to prove that it could not do anything but come to pass! Brother, even if you're the Benjamin in your family (the last of your class, the last to start the business, the last to create an enterprise, or the last to have a place in the market,) fear not! God can establish you as the head! He can take you from the bottom of the ladder where you are, to put you on top where all eyes can see you! Always remember it is God who promotes.

Certainly, there will be battles. It is not enough to accomplish the goal or attain the promise within a dream. You must continue to work and fight to see the promise in the earthly realm! It is also for this reason we are writing. Joseph's brothers dislike him, they even hated him **(Genesis 37:5)**, and even his father, despite his love for him, reproached him when he explained his dream to him **(Genesis 37:10)**. And hatred that his brothers had would push them to perform abominable acts to the common people against their brother Joseph. But for God, it was a strategy to accomplish His plan and His purpose.

The Mysteries of Divine Strategies

You know that our God is a God of order, and He does not think the way we think, "'For my thoughts are not your thoughts, neither are your ways my ways,' declares the LORD." **(Isaiah 55:8)**

On this basis, God does things that man cannot understand until the end. When he does things in the beginning, we complain, cry, and lament. In the end, we give Him all the glory and honor. The thought of God is deep and unfathomable. It is what I call the 'mysteries of divine strategies!

Take a deep look into the history of the Israelites, and you will understand that our God is a God of mystery! He gave to Joseph, one of the last-born of his father Jacob, the power and authority over his whole family. God is Sovereign! For this, his brothers did not like him and spoke to him with hatred! **(Genesis 37:4)** If I told you that it was God's plan, perhaps you would be surprised; and yet it is the truth! How could his brothers sell him if they did not hate him! They first wanted to take his life, "But they [the brothers of Joseph] saw him in the distance, and before he reached them, they plotted to kill him. 'Here comes that dreamer!' they said to each other. 'Come now, let's kill him and throw him into one of these cisterns and say that a ferocious animal devoured him. Then we'll see what comes of his dreams.'" **(Genesis 37:18-20)**

This is a way to show you the degree of their hatred!

But Joseph could not die without having accomplished his prophetic destiny! God will remove everything that is proposed of death by inspiring one of his older brothers named Ruben that will make another suggestion, "'Don't shed any blood. Throw him into this cistern here in the wilderness, but don't lay a hand on him.' Reuben said this to rescue him from them and take him back to his father." **(Genesis 37:22)**

The others complied with this word of Ruben and threw him into the pit. But it was planned for a very short time. Ruben wanted to deliver Joseph and to restore him to his father, which was not God's plan! The will of God was that Joseph should leave his family so that his dreams might be fulfilled; the will and the plan of God for him. So,

God, in His power, spared Joseph's life until the arrival of the Ishmaelites who had much earlier set out toward Egypt. Brother, God's ways are unfathomable, and yet, you cannot die without having been in the geographical location where your God will lift you; no matter how you arrive! Even if you have been sold or if you go as a slave, what is important is that you are in the location that God has prepared for you! Joseph's brothers sold him on the advice of Judah, "Judah said to his brothers, 'What will we gain if we kill our brother and cover up his blood? Come, let's sell him to the Ishmaelites and not lay our hands on him; after all, he is our brother, our own flesh and blood.' His brothers agreed. So when the Midianite merchants came by, his brothers pulled Joseph up out of the cistern and sold him for twenty shekels of silver to the Ishmaelites, who took him to Egypt." **(Genesis 37:26-28)**

Brother, bless God for everything that happens to you, even if you do not understand it. Joseph did not understand what was happening to him! He could have asked if God was really with him! I will answer for those who missed it, 'Yes.' God was with Joseph and he had a plan for him to be in Egypt and not in Midian.

It is for this reason that the Ishmaelites (or rather the Midianites) would sell him in Egypt, and to whom? To Potiphar, an officer of Pharaoh and captain of the guard. **(Genesis 37:36)** The invisible hand of the Creator was directing this whole thing! Yes, God was in control. It was His strategy at work for specific purposes. Joseph would breathe a little oxygen in the house of his master Potiphar before finding himself in a prison cell! It was a training from God to make him stronger and more powerful; specifically to get him closer to his destiny, King Pharaoh! It's true you can suffer from injustice; people can lie to put sticks in the wheels. You should remain faithful to God and you shall give Him all the glory. Raise your head high before your enemies.

Brother, to arrive in the big leagues, you must follow the normal path despite all the difficulties and trials that are there. All those who take dangerous shortcuts finish by slipping and missing the mark. You know that only the blessing of the LORD makes rich, and he adds no toil with it. **(Proverbs 10:22)**

Joseph took the path of divine blessing with all the thorns included. He refused to go with his master's wife and this led him to prison. He accepted to be rejected by men, knowing that he was approved by God! In this prison cell, God would send someone who was very close to King Pharaoh (namely his butler who served wine on his table). All these events were not accidental! To get Joseph closer to Pharaoh, God made the butler have a dream, which the young Hebrew would explain. Things happened as Joseph had said. In no time, Pharaoh also had a dream that nobody could explain. So, the butler who had resumed work remembered Joseph. And he was the one that God used to speak to Pharaoh about Joseph.

This is what I call **divine connections**!

You should never neglect them in spiritual warfare for God has always worked through connections. It took a young captive girl from Israel to talk about Elisha to her mistress, the wife of Naaman, the captain of the Syrian army before he was healed of his leprosy! **(2 Kings 5:1-19)** It took Naomi to talk about Boaz to Ruth for her to become his wife later; **(Ruth 3 & 4)**

To keep to these examples, do not neglect any connection that God gives us in our everyday life. In prison, Joseph did not minimize the butler of the king, he ministered to him instead. At that moment, Joseph got nothing.

Later, the butler of the king would talk about him to his master. Joseph would not only come out of the prison to explain the dream of Pharaoh- a dream that nobody could explain- but the king would again, obey his instructions. Joseph, by the hand of God, without having studied diplomacy found himself at the head of a foreign country. It was the beginning of the manifestation of divine strategies. In fact, what is it that we want to highlight? In His foreknowledge, God knew that a time would come when the famine would take over the whole world. The country he had chosen to provide food for others was Egypt. By doing so, the family of Jacob would not die of starvation, he strategically placed Joseph in Egypt to prepare the arrival of the family!

And that is what happened.

Joseph who was presented to the king, also presented his family to Pharaoh, who received them with open arms! "Pharaoh said to Joseph, 'Your father and your brothers have come to you, and the land of Egypt is before you; settle your father and your brothers in the best part of the land. Let them live in Goshen. And if you know of any among them with special ability, put them in charge of my own livestock.'" **(Genesis 47:5-6)**

God had not yet finished His plan, His strategy was at work! Israel could not perish; from a family, she was to become a powerful nation! This is the promise that God made to Jacob before he agreed to go down to Egypt, "'I am God, the God of your father,' he said. 'Do not be afraid to go down to Egypt, for I will make you into a great nation there.'" **(Genesis 46:3)**

And indeed, a family of seventy people, "With the two sons who had been born to Joseph in Egypt, the members of Jacob's family, which went to Egypt, were seventy in all." **(Genesis 46:27)** Israel became a mighty nation!

Their growing numbers troubled the new king Pharaoh who knew not Joseph. And he had bad thoughts toward the people, "Come, we must deal shrewdly with them or they will become even more numerous and, if war breaks out, will join our enemies, fight against us and leave the country." **(Exodus 1:10)** He would still tell midwives of the Hebrews, "When you are helping the Hebrew women during childbirth on the delivery stool, if you see that the baby is a boy, kill him; but if it is a girl, let her live." **(Exodus 1:16)**

However, despite all the atrocities of the king, God watched over His people and their number increased, **"But the more they were oppressed, the more they multiplied and spread; so the Egyptians came to dread the Israelites" (Exodus 1:12)** "The Israelites journeyed from Rameses to Sukkoth. There were about six hundred thousand men on foot, besides women and children."

213

(Exodus 12:37) God's plan for Israel was fulfilled: **enter Egypt as a family and came out as a nation.** Hallelujah!

At the beginning, Joseph did not understand the plan of God for his life. He certainly blamed his brother for the hatred they had for him. Maybe you're in the same boat. Brothers and sisters do you not understand why your parents failed to cover you with love! This is just because you are the "Joseph" of your family!

In divine strategies, God takes time to build his servants. With a house, the higher walls, the deeper and more solid the foundation must be. You do not become leader overnight. There are steps. There is what I call, 'the school of God' or 'the school of the Holy Spirit'! If you get with difficulty what others get easily, do not blame God. He knows what He is doing. Maybe you are a 'Joseph'. In His strategies, God is never in a hurry, but he is neither late, **He acts always in the time of His glory**, and at the right time. **(2 Corinthians 6:2; Isaiah 42:8)**

Also, in His strategies, to take Israel out of Egypt, God again chose someone; a newborn named Moses. King Pharaoh put to death all newly born Hebrew children. Moses was hidden by his mother for three months by the mighty Hand of the Lord. But after a while, she could not hide that big boy.

You ought to find another strategy! The invisible hand of the Creator is still at work. He will inspire his mother, "But when she could hide him no longer, she got a papyrus basket for him and coated it with tar and pitch. Then she placed the child in it and put it among the reeds along the bank of the Nile." **(Exodus 2:3)**

At first glance, one might think she went herself to hand over her son. She could be afraid that a wild animal could come to devour him or that ants come to bite him, etc. In her impotence before the cruelty of the king, she dropped her son, the fruit of her womb, at the bank of the river. But the child's sister stood at some distance to see what would happen to him. Nothing bad could happen to him whatever the thoughts crossing the mind of his mother and his sister. Why? Simply because the eyes of Jehovah watched over the child! It was not a case involving exclusively the family of Moses or of the Jews, Heaven was involved in this story! The moment the mother and sister of Moses finished playing their role, God entered the scene. It is in this moment, He awakened the spirit of the daughter of Pharaoh to come down to the river to bathe.

Certainly, her companions could have bad thoughts if they had discovered, this beautiful creature that is Moses before she did! God permitted that it should be the king's daughter herself that noticed the crate among the reeds. It is then her choice. She is the one who ordered her servant to fetch the crate! Once opened, she heard the child crying. In reality, it was the cry of destiny!

The child found grace in the eyes of the king's daughter, who had pity on him. This pity is not enough; it must manifest in compassion for something to be done in favor of the child. Automatically, God puts a suggestion in the mouth of the sister of the child, "Shall I go and get one of the Hebrew women to nurse the baby for you?" **(Exodus 2:7)** It was a question, but as far as I am concerned, it was an order from God. The princess had therefore neither time to calculate, nor to consider the reaction of her father Pharaoh, the supposed harbinger of the death of the little Hebrew, she could only agree, "'Go,' replied Pharaoh's daughter." And it is Moses' own mother who will not only take the child to breastfeed officially, but will again receive a salary.

"When the child grew older, she took him to Pharaoh's daughter and he became her son. She named him Moses, saying, 'I drew him out of the water.'" **(Exodus 2:10)**

Moses is going to receive Egyptian education; he will enter the practices and customs of Egypt, as if to say, **"When the LORD takes pleasure in anyone's way, he causes their enemies to make peace with them."** **(Proverbs 16:7)**

God had prepared the Egyptian, enemies of the Hebrews to train Moses, for he was the one who would later return to confront king Pharaoh so that Israel could be delivered and entered into its prophetic destiny.

Moses had everything to be a good Egyptian and live happily in a royal house. I'm sure that his clothing, language, and mannerisms reflected a good Egyptian, but his blood was Jewish! He could not ignore it, which was why God spared him from premature death and why he received a right education in a house that was so hostile to his race. It was God who had chosen him for this specific time to deliver Israel based on all the training, culture, habits, and language of the Egyptians that he had already mastered.

It was in this vein that Mordecai told Esther, when the people of Israel were threatened with death, "For if you remain silent at this time, relief and deliverance for the Jews will arise from another place, but you and your father's family will perish. And who knows but that you have come to your royal position for such a time as this?" **(Esther 4:14)**

Brothers and sisters, in divine strategies, God counted on one person that He lifted up, so that by his elevation, he could be a blessing to others. Do not forget your brothers and sisters and do not forget your friends of yesterday. Do not think that it is your strength, your intelligence, your know-how, or your relationships that have given you everything you have.

Remember that God was at the center of everything. Did he perhaps choose you so that you could save others? If you think about all that you endured and your suffering, you will not give a penny to anyone. You will be effectively stopping the Hand of God one way or another. There are good works which God prepared beforehand so that you practice them, "For we are God's handiwork, created in Christ Jesus to do good works, which God prepared in advance for us to do." **(Ephesians 2:10)**

People, practice good deeds. Do not look at the wicked and act according to their wickedness, but act according to the Word of God. My mother told me one day while I was angry against a lady who acted badly towards her, "My son, if you close your eyes to avoid seeing the passing of an evil person, a nice person who is your benefactor will pass unnoticed. Open your eyes and be serene."

Brothers and sisters, Moses opened his eyes and, despite all his comfort, preferred to choose to obey God.

And the divine strategy was that Moses went back to Egypt. He had fled after he killed an Egyptian who fought against one of his Jewish brothers. **(Exodus 2:11-15)** The battle was fierce; the new king Pharaoh had hardened his heart like a stone. However, Moses was able to bring the children of Israel out of Egypt by the grace of God and he was able to deliver them from slavery, "Then Moses said to the people, 'Commemorate this day, the day you came out of Egypt, out of the land of slavery, because the LORD brought you out of it with a mighty hand. Eat nothing containing yeast.'" **(Exodus 13:3)** Remember God used Joseph to bring His people in Egypt and used Moses to bring them out! He is a true strategist! He knows what He is doing.

A Success Produces Another Success

In the mysteries of divine strategies, God is always predictable. It is appropriate to recall that a success today must produce another success tomorrow. This is a string that should not stop. Who believes the all-knowing God does not know that Moses would not lead Israel to the Promised Land?

He certainly knew. It is for this reason, he prepared Joshua. And it was this young man who led Israel to the Promised Land; in a land flowing with milk and honey. Moses did not fight Joshua; nor did he seek to break him otherwise Joshua would have taken to his heel as David did before the threat of King Saul. Be like Moses who prepared Joshua and Elijah who prepared another successor, Elisha. Do like Paul who prepared Timothy and

God will be glorified. Listen to the word of the Lord, "After the death of Moses the servant of the LORD, the LORD said to Joshua son of Nun, Moses' aide: **'Moses my servant is dead.** Now then, you and all these people, *get ready to cross the Jordan River into the land I am about to give to them*—to the Israelites.'" **(Joshua 1:1-2)**

Moses knew by revelation, inspiration, or discernment that Joshua was with him prophetically. He invested in him and this is the young man who Moses could have neglected when he found that God had chosen him to fight the great kings before entering in their inheritance.

There are still today great kings who are opposed to the children of God who are preventing them from entering their inheritance. God has anointed Joshua to fight them, and help them. Do not fight them, and God's people will enter into their promised land. In these principles of the authority of God, obedience, respect, and submission to predecessors are imperative. This is not debatable! He who violates these principles may end up like the prodigal son who ended up with the swine. Water must not forget its source, otherwise it will dry up.

However, fathers and elders are to play their role to ensure that the young nursery can be tomorrow's success. A banana does not die without preparing its replacement! The fire does not go out without leaving a mark! The goat does not pass without leaving an odor. Prepare your 'Joshua'. This is part of the divine strategies! The Church of Jesus Christ is not a matter of ethnicity or a family issue. This is not a heritage that we bequeath to our families except by the edict of God. The Church of Jesus Christ is the Church of Jesus Christ, there is no alternative! There are no more Jews and there are no more Greek; we are one. Let us pray and God will reveal the 'Joshua' who will lead his people to their prophetic destiny!

When you refuse to obey the voice of God by choosing your own man instead of God's choice to lead the elect in their inheritance, you become a rebel to the will of the Creator. That is charismatic witchcraft!

Certainly, you preach God and you serve Him, but at the same time, you are against His interests; you mess up the strategies that He has put in place!

Repent and do it! Help someone. Invest yourself in them, listening to the voice of the Spirit for a success without a successor is a failure my Bible school teacher told me!

Jesus Christ, Our Lord of all, did not experience failure. He prepared His disciples before leaving the earth. He was very aware of the dramatic failure that the Church would suffer if He had not prepared successors.

He actually invested in twelve apostles and nobody was lost except the son of perdition! And among the twelve, there was one he chose as the head of the locomotive, which would draw the others. Clearly, he was the leader; This was Peter. Indeed, this man was like us and perhaps, even had a spiritual problem. When Jesus met him, he delivered him by breaking the influence of his name Simon (reed shaken by the wind) and by baptizing Cephas which means 'Stone'. **(John 1:42)**

It was in this 'reed' changed to 'rock' that Jesus Christ made this promise, "**And I tell you that you are Peter, and**

on this rock I will build my church, and the gates of Hades will not overcome it." (Matthew 16:18)

Jesus Christ had wrought many miracles and had made countless miracles, but He had not built a "physical" church.

The Church He built rather was spiritual and it was hidden in Peter. If Jesus Christ had no revelation to support Peter despite his mistakes and weaknesses, today maybe the Church would not exist.

There are 'Peters' who we should help to birth the Church that is hidden within them. When we speak of divine strategies, do not forget that the devil also has his ways to counteract or delay them. He inspired Joseph, the betrothed to Mary, to leave her so that she could be stoned according to the Law of Moses. But if Mary had died under stones, what becomes of her son Jesus? It was a strategy of the devil to prevent the birth of the Savior! And this strategy, Satan always applies to kill the chick in the egg. It is for us to carefully listen to God as Joseph did. He did not want a woman that he had not touched but was pregnant!

God applied another strategy; He would speak to Joseph in a dream, "Because Joseph her husband was faithful to the law, and yet did not want to expose her to public disgrace, he had in mind to divorce her quietly. But after he had considered this, an angel of the Lord appeared to him in a dream and said, 'Joseph son of David, do not be afraid to take Mary home as your wife, because what is conceived in her is from the Holy Spirit. She will give birth to a son, and you are to give him the name Jesus, because he will save his people from their sins.' All this took place to fulfill what the Lord had said through the prophet: 'The virgin will conceive and give birth to a son, and they will call him 'Immanuel' (which means 'God with us').' When Joseph woke up, he did what the angel of the Lord had commanded him and took Mary home as his wife." **(Matthew 1:19-24)**

Behold how by the obedience of Joseph, Satan failed. The same way, Satan wanted to kill the advent of the Church by crushing the one who was pregnant with it; Peter. But Jesus Christ quickly went into prayer for His spiritual son Simon Peter, "[And the Lord said,] 'Simon, Simon, Satan has asked to sift all of you as wheat. But I have prayed for you, Simon, that your faith may not fail. And when you have turned back, strengthen your brothers.'" **(Luke 22:31-32)**

Satan desired all the disciples to sift them as wheat, but Jesus Christ prayed for just one explicitly; the leader who was Peter. And He declared that the conversion of Peter is enough to strengthen the others. Jesus Christ did not accept that the leader and the bearer of the Church should die.

As if to say we should also distinguish our leaders established by God and by their elevation, we will in turn be strengthened and lifted.

Today, Satan demonstrates actions through his tricks! In fact, everyone acts as a leader; we do not know who does what and who is who? And it disturbs enormously divine strategies. No pastor wants to comply with the authority of the leaders appointed by God, so we are going from bad to worse.

Men of God are engaged in abominable things and nobody can correct them or put them on the right track because they think that they understand everything, they know everything. They divorce when they want, and they remarry when they want to; without good reason! They have second wives, mistresses, or women who take care of them and **they continue on preaching freely, a God they do not know**! I wonder what is the gospel they are preaching. Do they speak of the Holy One of Israel, or of another god? They forget that too much freedom kills freedom! We must all go through repentance.

Let us return to divine strategies and you will see that the Church will fulfill her role and people will need her. Our Heavenly Father is Himself a God of order that is why He gave the required capabilities to Peter who preached the first message after the departure of Jesus. And in his message, the leader (former reed shaken by the wind, now unshakable stone) defended the others, "These people are not drunk, as you suppose. It's only nine in the morning!" **(Acts 2:15)** There was no problem of leadership, the disciples recognized in Peter the man that God had established. It does not bring argument!

His faith and his tenacity supported the others and the Word of Jesus was accomplished on his life, "And I tell you that you are Peter, and on this rock I will build my church, and the gates of Hades will not overcome it." **(Matthew 16:18)**

Yes, by his preaching, the Church that Christ had put inside of him manifested herself in space and in time, "Those who accepted his message were baptized, and about three thousand were added to their number that day." **(Acts 2:41)** "All the believers were together and had everything in common." **(Acts 2:44)**

Brother, the success of Jesus did not stop at His death, or His ascension, but He rather revealed it in the lives of His disciples after His departure. We recognize the greatness of a man in what his son becomes. If you are rich or prosperous and you did not prepare a worthy heir, know that you worked unnecessarily. The blessing of Abraham spread on Isaac and that of Isaac on Jacob. Jacob's blessing fell on the twelve tribes of Israel. In the strategies of God, one glory must produce another glory and one success, another success. What we need to do is not cross our arms to criticize others or tear each other apart, but do the work in helping each other and relying on God. In the ministry or in all that we are doing as children of God, we must avoid doing politics of the belly or the system of 'divide and rule'. All of these things are based on ignorance. Buy knowledge freely and let's grow a little!

DO YOU KNOW THAT GOD HAS PREPARED EVERYTHING IN ADVANCE?

God, in His strategies, has prepared everything for His children. A father that the Lord has blessed gives each of his children the means, and all it takes for them to succeed in their life. The natural aides in explaining the spiritual and that leads me to say that Our Heavenly Father has prepared everything in advance! The problem is not God, it is we ourselves.

Learn to listen to His voice as He tells us in prayer, in dreams, in visions, or by His servants what we must do! Do not forget that blessing in the ministry or in business is geographical!

"The LORD had said to Abram, 'Go from your country, your people and your father's household to the land I will show you. I will make you into a great nation, and I will bless you; I will make your name great, and you will be a blessing. 3 I will bless those who bless you, and whoever curses you I will curse; and all peoples on earth will be blessed through you.'" **(Genesis 12:1-3)**

The geographical area where Abram was when he received the seven blessings contained in the promise; First, they would become a great nation, second, be blessed, third, have a great name, fourth, be a source of blessing, fifth, to bless those who bless him, sixth, to be a curse to those who curse him and finally, to have the seeds of blessing for all families of the earth-was not appropriate to his revelation.

It is for him to see these things in his life that God told him, "Get out and go where I will show you."

On the contrary, to Isaac, "The LORD appeared to Isaac and said, 'Do not go down to Egypt; live in the land where I tell you to live. Stay in this land for a while, and I will be with you and will bless you. For to you and your descendants I will give all these lands and will confirm the oath I swore to your father Abraham. I will make your descendants as numerous as the stars in the sky and will give them all these lands, and through your offspring all nations on earth will be blessed,'" **(Genesis 26:2-4)**

Isaac, in the strategy of God, should not leave Gerar, the country of the philistines, because it is the geographical area that God had prepared for his blessing! God had prepared everything in advance, he said, "For I know the plans I have for you," declares the LORD, "plans to prosper you and not to harm you, plans to give you hope and a future." **(Jeremiah 29:11)**

Despite the famine, Isaac obeyed the voice of God by staying in Gerar. He did not go down in Egypt. However, the seed that he made led him to wealth. "Isaac planted crops in that land and the same year reaped a hundredfold, because the LORD blessed him. The man became rich, and his wealth continued to grow until he became very wealthy." **(Genesis 26:12-13)**

If you know that God has prepared everything for you, stop doing wrong things. Earn your income honestly, work in the secret, and He will bless you publicly. I think this is what King David was saying to his son Solomon. "And you, my son Solomon, acknowledge the God of your father, and serve him with wholehearted devotion and with a willing mind, for the LORD searches every heart and understands every desire and every thought. If you seek him, he will be found by you; but if you forsake him, he will reject you forever. Consider now, for the LORD has chosen you to build a house as the sanctuary. Be strong and do the work." **(1 Chronicles 28:9-10)**

In this effort that Solomon must produce and in the acts which he must act on, do you think that this young man was abandoned to himself? No, his father, David, to whom God refused the construction of the temple to having been a man of war (or rather a soldier who shed blood) (**1 Chronicles 28:3**), prepared everything to facilitate the task to his son.

He first gave the model of the whole work as he has received from the Lord. (**1 Chronicles 28:11-19**) This is what I call 'vision'. We must have a clear vision of what we want to do. David received it well, "'All this,' David said, 'I have in writing as a result of the LORD's hand on me, and he enabled me to understand all the details of the plan.'" (**1 Chronicles 28:19**)

Being sure and confident that this vision was the emanation of God, he was not afraid, and he could not but encourage his son in relation to this work that he wanted to start, "David also said to Solomon his son, **'Be strong and courageous, and do the work. Do not be afraid or discouraged, for the LORD God, my God, is with you.** He will not fail you or forsake you until all the work for the service of the temple of the LORD is finished.'" (**1 Chronicles 28:20**)

After the vision of the model and the encouraging words, David provided everything needed to build the temple, "With all my resources I have provided for the temple of my God—gold for the gold work, silver for the silver, bronze for the bronze, iron for the iron and wood for the wood, as well as onyx for the settings, turquoise, stones of various colors, and all kinds of fine stone and marble—all of these in large quantities. Besides, in my devotion to the temple of my God I now give my personal treasures of gold and silver for the temple of my God, over and above everything I have provided for this holy temple: three thousand talents of gold (gold of Ophir) and seven thousand talents of refined silver, for the overlaying of the walls of the buildings, for the gold work and the silver work, and for all the work to be done by the craftsmen. Now, who is willing to consecrate themselves to the LORD today?" **(1 Chronicles 29:2-5)**

Brethren, this is what I called 'provision'. In the divine strategies, there is no disorder. He gives first the vision, then the encouraging words concerning the trials and difficulties that you will encounter. Finally, he sends the provision to achieve the vision. For someone who has received the vision, the provision is not doubted; he knows that God will provide. And this is what it was for Solomon who built the temple where his father told him,

"Then Solomon began to build the temple of the LORD in Jerusalem on Mount Moriah, where the LORD had appeared to his father David. It was on the threshing floor of Araunah the Jebusite, the place provided by David." **(2 Chronicles 3:1)**

God has made all things as did King David to his son Solomon. He put everything in front of you (materials, plan, model, location...) It is for you to know his will and to act accordingly. In acting you must know how to receive because there are also battle strategies that are not to be ignored.

The Mysteries of Battle Strategies

For a successful mission, a job well done, a ministry, or even one's own life, there are battle strategies to be adopted. We will reveal some to build the children of God.

To Be Committed to the Vision

Each of us has received a mission from God that he must accomplish on the earth. If you are a man of God, you must reveal God through the gifts he has put in you. If you are a politician, a craftsman, or whatever you are doing on earth, you have to reveal the God Who is in you. Clearly, each of us reveals God through what God gave us. Therefore, those who fail, fail for reasons that are clear; They are still attached to the gifts that God has given to the detriment of the Giver Himself. They accomplish no more the vision of God, but themselves their own vision. A branch detached from the trunk of a tree cannot but die. The same way, a detached vision of God will experience an abortion! The plan of the enemy is to stop us in our tracks, which is to accomplish the works of God on the earth; transforming this world in a positive way. God created it, but it is for us to transform it! So, if we remain attached to God, He will support us.

When the children of Israel (I would say the kingdom of Judah) sinned against God, Jeremiah the prophet said to them, "This whole country will become a desolate wasteland, and these nations will serve the king of Babylon seventy years." **(Jeremiah 25:11)** This prophetic message was fulfilled in **2 Chronicles 36:11-21**. The wrath of God struck the people and those who did not die by the sword of the king of the Chaldeans, were made captives in Babylon until the completion of seventy years. After that, God would deliver his people after the prayers of His servant Daniel. **(Daniel 9)** But leaving Babylonian exile is made with three figureheads; Zerubbabel, Ezra and Nehemiah. The vision that God gave to each of these three main characters is different from each other.

Indeed, Zerubbabel who came out with the first wave came with a vision to rebuild the temple of God. And this order to build the temple came from God himself because after Daniel's prayer, God awakened the spirit of the one who had the authority to liberate Judah to accomplish this mission; Cyrus, king of Persia, "In the first year of Cyrus king of Persia, in order to fulfill the word of the LORD spoken by Jeremiah, the LORD moved the heart of Cyrus king of Persia to make a proclamation throughout his realm and also to put it in writing: 'This is what Cyrus king of Persia says: 'The LORD, the God of heaven, has given me all the kingdoms of the earth and he has appointed me to build a temple for him at Jerusalem in Judah. Any of his people among you may go up, and may the LORD their God be with them.''" **(2 Chronicles 36:22-23)**

God began by His temple to show us that God must always be in the first place. Zerubbabel (with those whom God has awakened their spirit) built the temple of God. There was a stop which lasted fifteen years due to fierce opposition, but Zerubbabel remained committed to the vision of his Heavenly Father! The consequence is that the vision of the building of the house of the Lord was fulfilled, "So the elders of the Jews continued to build and prosper under the preaching of Haggai the prophet and Zechariah, a descendant of Iddo. They finished building the temple according to the command of the God of Israel and the decrees of Cyrus, Darius and Artaxerxes, kings of Persia. The temple was completed on the third day of the month Adar, in the sixth year of the reign of King Darius." **(Ezra 6:14-15)**

After the construction of the temple, Ezra came with another vision; to rebuild the people themselves. Indeed, the temple was certainly built, but the people were distorted because of sin. To be identified anew to God, it was imperative to go through sanctification. It is this vision- this work- that God will have entrusted to Ezra! He in turn remained attached to the heavenly vision, "For Ezra had devoted himself to the study and observance of the Law of the LORD, and to teaching its decrees and laws in Israel." **(Ezra 7:10)**

Remaining committed to the vision, he was able to bring the people back to God; the people who not only turned away but had also separated to foreign women who lived in abomination.

The mission can grow, it can even be modified, but it should never be neglected nor abandoned. When Ezra remained committed to the vision, the whole nation followed him and complied with his word! "While Ezra was praying and confessing, weeping and throwing himself down before the house of God, a large crowd of Israelites—men, women and children—gathered around him. They too wept bitterly. Then Shekaniah son of Jehiel, one of the descendants of Elam, said to Ezra, 'We have been unfaithful to our God by marrying foreign women from the peoples around us. But in spite of this, there is still hope for Israel. Now let us make a covenant before our God to send away all these women and their children, in accordance with the counsel of my lord and of those who fear the commands of our God. Let it be done according to the Law.'" **(Ezra 10:1-3)**

What a transformation! Hallelujah!

The temple was built and the people reconciled with God. Nehemiah would come with another vision; to build or reconstruct the wall. This was the third departure. You see that our God is a God of order, and that each generation has a specific mission; mission whose rules are set by God Himself! When we look deeply and are warned on these three waves and those three persons used by God, we understand that God was doing through them, a work in progress. It is God who fulfills His vision through the channels He has chosen. But what is exciting and interesting is that each of these three people took this work as his own! They were identified to God to affect His people positively. Their hearts beat in the rhythm of the heart of God; they had a vision that they really wanted to accomplish. The walls of Nehemiah symbolized protection and security. It was guaranteed, as if to say when we do the things of God and we live a life according to His word, God is 'obliged' to protect us. He cannot remain silent; He most imperatively protects us. This wall is also a picture of an endogenous possession; inside of us, we are convinced of our physical and spiritual security. We do not fear! This is what God does with His children.

Nehemiah could not sleep or eat when he learned about the state of the wall of Jerusalem, "They said to me, "Those who survived the exile and are back in the province are in great trouble and disgrace. **The wall of Jerusalem is broken down, and its gates have been burned with fire."** **4 When I heard these things, I sat down and wept. For some days I mourned and fasted and prayed before the God of heaven." (Nehemiah 1:3-4)**

Brother are you touched by the state of your church and the Church in general. Are you concerned with the work of God like Nehemiah? Nothing is done to the advancement of God's work except to protect the interests of the Church.

Everyone thinks about himself and his own interests! Wherever you are, if you're a man chosen by God to fulfill a heavenly vision, you cannot escape! Despite the presence of Nehemiah in the house of the king Artaxerxes serving for the table, the vision of the work was to lead Nehemiah in a geographical area where he had to accomplish a mission. And that is what happened, Nehemiah was able to build the wall of Jerusalem!

However, we must recognize that this vision was fought, just like that of Zerubbabel. There were mountains of oppositions, but they remained faithful not only to God but also (and especially) to the vision He had given them. These are battle strategies that discourage Satan and his demons. When one focuses on the vision and remains positive confessing that God will do it always, Satan is enraged, because he sees his failure. Remain committed to the vision, even if Sanballat or Tobiah rises. **(Nehemiah 4:1-39)** Do as Nehemiah and his companions, "…Those who carried materials did their work with one hand and held a weapon in the other, and each of the builders wore his sword at his side as he worked. But the man who sounded the trumpet stayed with me." **(Nehemiah 4:17-18)** Work without forgetting to arm ourselves and being ready for battle.

To Be Armed With Strategic Prayers

We cannot be successful in a work on earth without prayer. If you refuse to pray to the true God, you will be obliged to pray the little gods of nature which are incomparable or even close to the God of creation. While you work, complete the work of God, or while you do business, never neglect the mysteries of strategies in battle. Many people have underestimated them, and have not seen their projects or dreams come to pass.

In everything you do, arm yourself with strategic prayer. The companions of Nehemiah worked with one hand and held in the other, weapons of battle. I would rather say 'weapons of strategic prayer'.

Pray these few prayers with me,

• "Lord God, Creator of all the universe, look at all the earth, locate all my enemies who come together in my name, and scatter them in the name of Jesus. Lord, in the same way that you confused the language of human beings during the construction of the Tower of Babel, confound the language of my enemies so they will not agree concerning me. Let confusion be their potion in the name of Jesus! Turn their backs against one another and scatter them by the power of your Spirit in Jesus' name." **(Genesis 11:1-9)**

• "Lord, I stand in your Blood and I declare that any army assembled against me be smitten with blindness in the Name of Jesus! Elisha prayed and the Syrians were struck with blindness. **(2 Kings 6:18)** the angels of God prayed and struck with blindness the inhabitants of Sodom and Gomorrah who came to the door with intent to hurt them. **(Genesis 19:11)** Apostle Paul prayed until obscurity and darkness fell upon Elymas the magician. **(Acts 13:9-11)** I also pray the same prayer; Lord take away sight from my enemies. Cover their eyes with darkness so they will not be able to see my happiness and fight against it. I want it and I declare it in the name of Jesus!"

• "Lord, I stop the sun at the place where my enemies were located and I avenge them in the name of Jesus. Joshua stopped the sun and the moon to take vengeance on Israel's enemies; I will do the same by the power of the Holy Spirit!"

• "Lord God, how long shall my glory be outraged? Arise, O LORD my God, save me! As you hit the cheek of all my enemies, you break the teeth of the wicked in the name of Jesus! **(Psalm 3:8)**"

• "Heavenly Father, regardless of the fiery furnace in which I was thrown, my home, my family, my business, my finances, my relationships, and my qualifications; we all come out of this furnace as Daniel's three companions in the name of Jesus! And I declare that the heat of the furnace which they themselves have lit devours them in the Name of Jesus!" **(Daniel 3:22, 27)**

•"I'm also going to war against my accusers; I stand up against them so that they themselves fall into the lions' den. Lord, Daniel was removed from the lions' den where his enemies and his accusers threw him. In return, they too were thrown into the same den and the lions ate them. I come out, in the name of Jesus, from every den and I throw all my accusers in it in the name of Jesus!" **(Daniel 6:23-24)**

•"Close the mouths of lions that physically or spiritually rise up against me. Send your angel to close their mouths in the name of Jesus! **(Daniel 6:22)** They will not be able to harm me, as they did not succeed to harm Daniel when he was with them in the den, in the Name of Jesus!"

•"Now Lord, I dispose my enemies favorable to me in Jesus' Name! **(Proverbs 16:7)** Lord, in the same way that you used the Egyptians so that they gave the children of Israel jewels of silver and vessels of gold and clothing, use my enemies. **(Exodus 12:35)** Lord God, the same way you shamed Haman and used him to lift Mordecai whom he hated, favorably use all my enemies without exception in the Name of Jesus!" **(Esther 6:4-12)**

•"Lord, as it was necessary that when the king could not sleep, for him to remember nothing else besides reading the annals and the chronicles of the good deeds of Mordecai **(Esther 6:1-3)**, it was also necessary that king Darius could not sleep until the release of Daniel from the lions' den. **(Daniel 6:18)** In the same way, take away the sleep of all my benefactors so that they can become a blessing for me. If they sleep, they may not remember me, Lord. Wake them and wake up their spirit as you awakened the spirit of King Cyrus to rebuild the temple in Jerusalem. **(Ezra 1:1-3)** Lord, let him who you have prepared for my elevation be lifted so that I too can be lifted. He should not sleep until he does what he has to do for me, so that I can enter my prophetic destiny in the name of Jesus!"

• "Lord, I take by the power of your Spirit what I missed or that which was stolen from me in the name of Jesus. Your word says that I received something from heaven which is mine. **(John 3:27)** It is my "Star! But there is a thief which comes to steal (John 10: 10) and today I declare that all my happiness, my grace, my greatness, my fame, and my possessions which were stolen, taken, or that are fallen, come back to me in Jesus' Name! When the iron that was used to cut the wood fell into the water, Elisha the prophet cut a piece of wood, threw it in the water, and the iron began to float. He said to his spiritual son, "Take it!" And he put forth his hand, and took it. **(2 Kings 6:1-7)**

I also stretch my hand and I take back everything that belongs to me that fell or was lost! I take back my star and I shine in the name of Jesus!"

• "Father Creator, purify the source of my life in the name of Jesus. Your servant Elisha by his prayer purified the source of the water of Jericho which produced death and barrenness. I too, on this day by prayer, Lord, purify the sources of my life, communicate flavor where they put bitterness, give life where there is death and my life will never be barren again! I want to be productive in the name of Jesus." **(2 Kings 2:19-22)**

• "Lord, give me the nations for inheritance. Help me possess the ends of the earth for the glory of your name! **(Psalm 2:8)** I possess by the power of your word everywhere the soles of my feet shall tread upon in the name of Jesus! **(Joshua 1:3)** And it's for your goals Lord! (All our prayers must take into account the interests of God and not exclusively ours. This was the case of Hannah who prayed to have a child that she would devote to God all his life. **(1 Samuel 1:10-12)** Esther prayed for his people and Daniel interceded for deliverance of his people from the Babylonian captivity. **(Daniel 9)** Jesus prayed to ask for the kingdom and the will of God on earth. And after our various prayers, always give thanks to the Lord, say thank you because by faith we know that we are answered!) Thank you Lord for answering me, let your name be glorified! Amen!"

Brothers and sisters, here are some examples of strategic prayers among many others you can pray. But what we want to emphasize is the importance of commitment to the vision sustained by prayer and the importance of acting according to the vision.

Act According to the Vision or Construct Aligned to Divine Dimensions

Remember one can remain attached to the vision before starting it and change it later by the nature of things. This means that there is a difference between being committed to a vision and acting on it. I pray the Lord help us not only to remain committed to the vision, but also to act on it. All should be as God said; that everything be done according to the scriptures. On the evening of your life and the evening of your ministry, all your work should be the exact photocopy of what God has said. We saw it with Moses, servant of God. He received orders concerning the tabernacle that he was to build in honor of Jehovah God. And at the end of his work, the Bible tells us, "The Israelites had done all the work just as the LORD had commanded Moses. 43 Moses inspected the work and saw that they had done it just as the LORD had commanded. So Moses blessed them." **(Exodus 39:42-43)**

It is Moses who received the vision and he is the one God gave orders to. So, he must lead and ensure that nothing changes vis-à-vis what he received from God!

Brother do not oppose a man of God who has a divine mandate. Your role is to give him advice, encouragement, and support so that he can fulfill the vision that God gave him. Each brings his share but it rests upon the servant to ensure that the people and all the workers act in accordance to the vision! After drawing up the tabernacle, the Bible tells us in chapter 40 of Exodus more than eight times that, *"Moses did all that the LORD commanded him, so did he,"* or, *"as... the LORD commanded Moses."*

This is what God wants each of his children to do; that the scripture might be fulfilled in our lives. And if you act and build according to the dimensions of God at the end of your work, the cloud will surely cover your work and the glory of the Lord shall rest upon you! This is the coronation of your ministry! This is what happened with

Moses when he dressed the tabernacle, "Then a cloud covered the tent of meeting, and the glory of the LORD filled the tabernacle." **(Exodus 40:34)** "So the cloud of the LORD was over the tabernacle by day, and fire was in the cloud by night, in the sight of all the Israelites during all their travels." **(Exodus 40:38)**

If you do a work inspired by God and there is neither cloud nor glory at the end, ask yourself questions. Is it that you modified or changed the dimensions? This is the sign to know whether you have acted according to the vision or not! Know with God, we cannot cheat. He is the most supreme judge, who pronounces the verdict and cannot be wrong, "With me are riches and honor, enduring wealth and prosperity." **(Proverbs 8:18)**

Therefore, He is ready to give great glory to His children who remain faithful in their actions. However, it is not always easy to remain committed to a vision and act on this vision. When God told Noah to build the ark, it took not only time, but also required a lot of effort and courage! It was not easy at all but Noah did not change the divine prescriptions. Read the Word of God, "So God said to Noah, 'I am going to put an end to all people, for the earth is filled with violence because of them. I am surely going to destroy both them and the earth. So make yourself an ark of cypress wood; make rooms in it and coat it with pitch inside and out. This is how you are to build it: The ark is to be three hundred cubits long, fifty cubits wide and thirty cubits high. Make a roof for it, leaving below the roof an opening one cubit high all around. Put a door in the side of the ark and make lower, middle and upper decks.'" **(Genesis 6:13-16)**

God, in His sovereignty, knew why He gave all these details to Noah:

-Make an ark of gopher wood

-You arrange its cells

-You plaster it with pitch inside and outside

-You shall make a window in the ark

-You shall set a door on the side of the ark

-You shall build a lower floor, a second, and a third.

Noah had his destiny before him and God played his role in giving him the vision. It is left for him to build the ark according to the vision without changing anything. If he had made changes, it could have been fatal to him and his family. The vision that you have received is to save not just you, but also your whole family, a village, a city, a country, a generation... you may have been called to save nations. Do not joke with all the details that God gave you. Noah was to take the wood "gopher" to build the ark, for God in His foreknowledge knew that the flood would last forty days and the waters would be upon the Earth for one hundred fifty days. **(Genesis 7:17, 24)** It was necessary that the wood resist moisture. It should not rot and there should be no damage. Moreover, it was also necessary to have the 'pitch' inside and outside as to prevent water infiltration.

God had it all planned!

At the cellular level, they were prepared to accommodate the different species of animals which were to come into the ark to escape the flood and ensure their survivability. The door on the side of the ark was to lead them inside but to facilitate their work, God asked Noah to build a stage of three levels. Maybe Noah, you, and I fail to understand why God gave these instructions. But in the end, Noah glorified God. Even the window in this time of flood, had its role; it allowed Noah to release first a raven, then the dove to see the water level and gauge whether the earth dried up. **(Genesis 7:6-12)**

If Noah had not acted according to the dimensions given by God, and he did not build the ark with the cell, many animals would not have entered into the ark, and would have disappeared in the flood or been crushed by the larger ones.

If Noah had chosen another timber to defray cost in exchange of strength, or had not coated the ark in pitch, perhaps the worst would have happened and God would have had to restart another creative work. But by his obedience, Noah was able to keep every animal and every living creature according to its kind including himself, the human being!

Brother, how are you building your life, your ministry, your business; according to God's dimension or with fraud and falsehood? Be careful to not mock God, for what you sow, you shall reap. **(Galatians 6:7)** Some things are certain; there will be rain, there will be the flood, and waters will be large on the earth but what we cannot certify is the resistance of your ark! Can your ark withstand all these calamities? Can your ark be above the water and float to the place indicated by God? If there is a blockage, review your life to seek the origin and seek for deliverance.

Daniel Buraimo

Conclusion

Brothers and sisters, the love I have for you does not allow me to tell you untruths, but to tell you only the truth. Many religions are born and continue to born. There is an overabundance of doctrines, methods, and practices that have nothing to do with the true gospel. **This is the trick of the devil to keep the children of God from the wonderful name of Jesus.**

Spiritual warfare is imperative. It is not just the material realm that warfare engages! Because of the goods of this world that Satan offers, many do not try to discern. They worship an unknown god! Their sole purpose is to be well on the earth and they will tell you that Heaven is a fiction to console people in their error! The evangelist Matthew asks us a question, "What good will it be for someone to gain the whole world, yet forfeit their soul? Or what can anyone give in exchange for their soul?" **(Matthew 16:26)**

Brother, you may have been in error, to err is human. But following an endless road or any specific destination is another story and the trick of the enemy. You can still catch up by making a U-turn. Do not persist in error while the truth has been revealed to you. Jesus said, "**Then you will know the truth, and the truth will set you free."** **(John 8:32)**

Let the truth set you free before it is too late. It is one thing to know the truth and another thing entirely to let it set you free. The truth is that Jesus is the One whom God sent from heaven to lead mankind in the heavenly city. And His death was included in the plan of God for our salvation. I repeat these words because there are some religions that do not believe in the death of Jesus,

"We really killed the Messiah, Jesus, son of Mary, the Messenger of Allah... **But they did neither kill nor crucified, but it was a sham." (Surah 4:157)** Blasphemy!

What then was the passion of Jesus?

Were the last three months of His life forgotten by this religion? If there had not been a crucifixion, can we speak of His resurrection; one of the foundations of the Christian faith?

Jesus was crucified!

There are even extra-biblical texts that confirm to us the truth and the veracity of the information that is the biblical declaration. At the historical level, the life and the death of Jesus are attested and took place in the reported space and in the time. Historians PLINE LE JEUNE, TACITE, FLAVIUS, JOSEPHE, SUETONE, LUCIEN and TERTULLEN mentioned Jesus and the primitive church.

They spoke of His death and resurrection without a shadow of doubt!

The book, *History of Mankind Volume II Antiquity* (1200 before Jesus to 500 AD) tells us about Jesus' execution, which took place the 14th of the month of Nisan (which corresponds a little to our month of March) probably in 30 AD in a place called Golgotha. This is specifically in the section entitled "Jesus and His work, the origins of Christianity" on page 732.

The Bible does not say otherwise, it actually confirms it, **"Jesus bearing his cross, went forth into a place called the place of a skull, which is called in the Hebrew Golgotha." (John 19:17-18 KJV)** This is where He was crucified and the place was not even hidden, please! **This is why many people could read what the king Pilate had written, 'JESUS OF NAZARETH THE KING OF THE JEWS.' Many of the Jews read this sign, for the place where Jesus was crucified was near the city, and the sign was written in Aramaic, Latin and Greek." (John 19:20)**

Satan has (unfortunately by trickery) kept people in religiosity while their sins remained unforgiven because they did not accept that the Blood of Jesus was shed for them.

Outside this group, there are other people who worship idols which were given religious names. They took pleasure in these things. No, God does not give His glory to another, nor His honor to idols. **(Isaiah 42:8) An idol is an idol; a statue is a statue; whatever name we give it.** For example, the statue of the angel Gabriel is not the angel Gabriel. As soon as you remove the name Gabriel, there remains only the statue. If you are worshipping, it is this statue you worship! There is no difference between you and the old idolaters, who worshipped the sacred wood in the forest. Suffer to be shocked and saddened so that you can be saved rather than remain in the religion and find yourself in the great tribulation or in hell! I know one thing, godly sorrow lead to repentance and salvation, while worldly sorrow leads to death. **(2 Corinthians 7:10)** This was the case of Judas! Be saddened by God and come back home to your Father in true repentance and true worship. Together we can meet at the same table as the Lord with Abraham, Elijah, Moses, and the others. It will be wonderful and I refuse that you will be absent. Accept therefore these truths and advance into the deep water with the Lord.

Brother, God is Spirit and we must worship Him in spirit. This is the reason Satan, with the intention to eliminate the true Christianity, martyred the disciples of Jesus who worshiped Him in spirit. At Ephesus for example, the true Gospel was used to snatch the people from religion in favor of true worship. It was a public outcry because **their manufacturing industry of temples of the goddess Diana was due to experience bankruptcy! (Acts 19:24-28)**

This is an industry and this is idolatry! If you want to worship God, worship Him; do not mix Him with the other strange gods. The queen of heaven holds men in captivity and closes their eyes to the truth of the Gospel. She makes God to be seen in female form just to make people worship her! It is a terrible demon and worshiped in many countries of the world. God in his anger said to Jeremiah the prophet, "So do not pray for this people nor offer any plea or petition for them; do not plead with me, for I will not listen to you. Do you not see what they are doing in the towns of Judah and in the streets of Jerusalem? **The children gather wood, the fathers light the fire, and the women knead the dough and make cakes to offer to the Queen of Heaven. They pour out drink offerings to other gods to arouse my anger."** **(Jeremiah 7:16-18)**

The entire family worships this demon to anger God and He asks his servant not to pray for such people! The queen of heaven (as her name indicates) appears sometimes in the first heaven to keep men in religious captivity and spiritual slavery. She is a first-class agent of Satan. She makes people live in abomination and in orgies (in total depravity and) attempts to make the true gospel insensible. Her followers do not consider sin as such, and she gives semblance prosperity! **(Jeremiah 44:16-22)**

She likes riots, argument, blood flow, and rebellions; especially when the truth is preached. **(Acts 19:23-38; Nahum 3:1-4)** She fights the saints, and feeds on their blood in order to discourage them from their mission **(Revelation 17:1-6)** We must open our eyes and have discernment!

There are places of worship where Satan sits as the supreme master. He rules and reigns because of the presence and the worship of idols, as well as the people who are unaware of the reality of spiritual warfare. To keep people in spiritual bondage, he performs miracles like the sorcerers and magicians did in Egypt before Moses and King Pharaoh. But in reality, it was not God! God is clear when he wants His voice to be heard, "**I am the LORD; that is my name! I will not yield my glory to another or my praise to idols.**" (Isaiah 42:8)

And finally, there are those who worship the devil outright through certain names, religious leaders, or other means. Also there are those who say they are atheists.

To all these different types of groups, I want to tell you just one thing; come back to Jesus Christ. Hear this word of the Lord, "**Therefore, 'Come out from them and be separate,' says the Lord. 'Touch no unclean thing, and I will receive you.' And, 'I will be a Father to you, and you will be my sons and daughters,' says the Lord Almighty.**" (2 Corinthians 6:17-18) What a word so strong and wonderful!

Do not play with the Word of God. Jesus reiterates, "Look, I am coming soon! Blessed is the one who keeps the words of the prophecy written in this scroll." (Revelation 22:7) **"Look, I am coming soon! My reward is with me, and I will give to each person according to what they have done." (Revelation 22:12) "I, Jesus, have sent my angel to give you this testimony for the churches. I am the Root and the Offspring of David, and the bright Morning Star." (Revelation 22:16)**

The time is closer now than ever before, it is time to seek the Lord. This is why it was recommended to John not to seal the words of the prophecy of the book of Revelation **(22:10)**

Jesus is coming, be vigilant!
Can we say together, Amen!
Come, Lord Jesus.

Contact us

By Phone:

USA 1 (863) 670-2096

Ivory Coast (001) 07274959

Whatsapp +1 863 670-2096

By E-mail:

Simiudaniel@yahoo.com

About The Author

Prophet BURAIMO SIMIU *(Daniel)* is a husband and father. He is the president and founder of Mission PENIEL International that maintains offices in Cote d'Ivoire and the USA.

Prophet BURAIMO SIMIU is a trainer, and intercessor as well as a divinely inspired writer. He received his training under Bishop Paul Simplice Kouadio of International Mission of Evangelization and at Institut LIFE in the USA. Prophet BURAIMO SIMIU has been ordained as a prophet by Apostle Marilynn J. Davis, President and Founder of Shekinah Tabernacle in the USA.

www.ingramcontent.com/pod-product-compliance
Lightning Source LLC
Chambersburg PA
CBHW020607270326
41927CB00005B/208